D1609041

the Answer Book for

a simple approach to
Old Testament
HEBREW

Ethelyn Simon, Nanette Stahl, Linda Motzkin, Joseph Anderson

Consultant to the Authors: Professor Jacob Milgrom
Professor of Hebrew and Bible, Department of Near Eastern Studies
University of California at Berkeley

Assistant Consultant: Kenneth Shoemaker

©1981 by EKS Publishing Company
ISBN 0-939144-04-2

This answer book is designed to accompany

A Simple Approach to Old Testament Hebrew

(ISBN 0-939144-03-4).

It can be ordered directly from EKS Publishing Company,
or through your favorite bookstore.

This **Answer Book** provides complete answers for all exercises in **A Simple Approach to Old Testament Hebrew**, a textbook designed to introduce this ancient language as easily as possible. These answers will help the teacher correct all written work, and the student correct himself as he studies.

In order to make this study as easy as possible, we have chosen to make all translations into English as literal as possible. We have translated the Hebrew word for word within the bounds of correct though sometimes awkward English.

EKS Publishing Company

Office Address	Mailing Address
5336 College Avenue	P.O. Box 11133
Oakland, California 94618	Oakland, California
415-653-5183	94611-0133

CHAPTER 1

Exercise 4A 1. א,ב,ג,ד 2. ה,ו,ז 3. ו,ז,ח 4. א,ב,ג,ד,ה
5. ד,ה,ו,ז,ח

Exercise 4B 1. ט,י,כ 2. ל,מ,נ 3. ט,י,כ,ל,מ,ן 4. ד,ה,ו,
ז,ח,ט,י,ך,ל 5. א,ב,ג,ד,ה,ו,ז,ח,ט,י,כ,ל,מ

Exercise 4C 1. ס,ע,פ,צ 2. ק,ר,שׂ,ת 3. ס,ע,פ,ץ 4. ס,ע,פ,
צ,ק,ר,שׂ,ת

Exercise 6C 1. פ 2. שׂ 3. ע,צ,ר,ת 4. מ,ס,צ,ק,ר,ת 5. ז,
ח,י,ל,מ,פ,צ,ר,ת 6. ד,ו,ז,ט,י

Exercise 7C א,ה,ח,ע,ר

Exercise 8C ב,ג,ד,כ,פ,ת

Exercise 9C כ-ך,מ-ם,נ-ן,פ-ף,צ-ץ

Exercise 1D 1. resh - daleth 2. aleph - tsadhe 3. yodh -
waw 4. beth - kaf 5. cheth - taw 6. mem - teth 7. nun -
gimmel 8. hey - cheth 9. waw - final nun 10. nun - kaf
11. zayin - waw 12. tsadhe - ayin 13. daleth - final kaf
14. final mem - samech 15. zayin - daleth

Exercise 2D א,ע

Exercise 3D ט,ף

Exercise 4D כ,ק

Exercise 5D אב, בחר, גאל, דרך, הנה, ור, זקן, חטא, טוב, יד,
כל, למה, מות, נתן, עלה, פנים, צד, קול, רק, שׂמים, תורה

CHAPTER 2

Exercise 3A 1. מָוֶת 2. עֵוֶר 3. וַתָּקָם 4. דָּוִד

Exercise 4A 1. קַיִם 2. מַיִם 3. יָלַד 4. בַּיִת 5. יֵשׁ

Exercise 5A ב,ת,ח,ג,ב,פ,ד,כ

1

Exercise 6A   ע,ר,ח,ה,ה,ר,א,ה,ח,ח,ע,ר,א,ה

Exercise 2B   1. דּור   2. לָמָה   3. אֹכֶל   4. אֵם   5. תָּמָר

Exercise 4B   1. sheets   2. seen   3. zoom   4. key   5. yacht
6. goat   7. doze   8. lone   9. cave   10. deaf   11. rate
12. oats   13. name   14. car   15. loom   16. tell   17. tar
18. two   19. ooze

CHAPTER 3

Exercise 2   1. בָּ/נוֹת   2. מֵ/חִים   3. שָׁ/פַט   4. נָ/שׁוּב

5. אָכְ/לֹב   6. אַבְ/רָ/הָם   7. אֶ/רֶץ   8. יִכְ/תְּבוּ   9. הוֹ/לְ/כֶת

10. יַ/עֲ/קֹב

Exercise 3   1. short-sound   2. silent   3. both   4. silent
5. short-sound

Exercise 4   1. כָּתַב   2. גּוּר   3. אֶזְכֹּר   4. דּוֹד   5. בָּרוּךְ

6. פָּקַד   7. מְאֹד   8. פָּנָי

Exercise 5   אָלֶף, בֵּית, גִּמֶּל, דָּלֶת, הֵא, וָו, זַיִן, חֵית, טֵית, יוֹד,
כַּף, לָמֶד, מֵם, נוּן, סָמֶךְ, עַיִן, פֵּא, צָדִי, קוֹף, רֵישׁ, שִׁין, תָּו

CHAPTER 4

Exercise 1   1. A. זָכַר   B. זָכַר דָּוִד   C. זָכַר נַעַר   D. זָכַר הוּא

2. A. הוּא הָלַךְ   B. הוּא זָכַר   E. זָכַר יַעֲקֹב   F. זָכַר בֹּעַז   אַבְרָהָם

C. הוּא פָּתַב

1. Boaz remembered.   A. David remembered.   B. A lad...
C. He...   D. Abraham...   E. Jacob...   F. Boaz...   2. He wrote.
A. He went.   B. ...remembered.   C. ...wrote.

Exercise 2   1. Boaz remembered.   2. Abraham went.   3. A man
wrote.   4. A lad remembered.   5. Jacob wrote.   6. He walked.
7. David remembered.   8. He wrote.   9. Abraham remembered.

Exercise 3   בֹּעַז, זָכַר, אַבְרָהָם, הָלַךְ, פָּתַב, יַעֲקֹב, דָּוִד

Exercise 4   בֹּעַז, זָכַר, אַבְרָהָם, הָלַךְ, אִישׁ, נַעַר, יַעֲקֹב, הוּא

2

Exercise 5 1. אַבְרָהָם זָכַר or זָכַר אַבְרָהָם. 2. אִישׁ הָלַךְ or הָלַךְ

אִישׁ. 3. הוּא הָלַךְ... 4. זָכַר דָּוִד... 5. כָּתַב בֹּעַז... 6. נַעַר הָלַךְ...

Exercise 6 1. דָּוִד כָּתַב. 2. הָלַךְ נַעַר. 3. אַבְרָהָם זָכַר. 4. הוּא

הָלַךְ. 5. יַעֲקֹב כָּתַב.

1. David wrote. 2. A lad went. 3. Abraham remembered. 4. He
went. 5. Jacob wrote.

CHAPTER 5

Exercise 1 1. A. רוּת כָּתְבָה. B. נַעֲרָה כָּתְבָה. C. הִיא כָּתְבָה.

D. שָׂרָה כָּתְבָה. E. מִשְׁפָּחָה כָּתְבָה. F. הַנַּעֲרָה כָּתְבָה. 2. A. אַבְרָהָם

הָלַךְ. B. דָּוִד הָלַךְ. C. הוּא הָלַךְ. D. הָאִישׁ הָלַךְ. E. בֹּעַז הָלַךְ.

F. הַנַּעַר הָלַךְ. 3. A. רוּת כָּתְבָה סֵפֶר. B. אַבְרָהָם כָּתַב סֵפֶר. C. הָאִשָּׁה

כָּתְבָה... D. בֹּעַז כָּתַב... E. הַנַּעֲרָה כָּתְבָה... F. יַעֲקֹב כָּתַב...

G. הַנַּעַר כָּתַב... H. הַמִּשְׁפָּחָה כָּתְבָה...

1. The woman wrote. A. Ruth wrote. B. A maiden wrote.
C. She wrote. D. Sarah wrote. E. A family wrote. F. The
maiden wrote. 2. Jacob went. A. Abraham went. B. David
went. C. He went. D. The man went. E. Boaz went. F. The lad
went. 3. Naomi wrote a book. A. Ruth wrote a book.
B. Abraham wrote a book. C. The woman wrote... D. Boaz
wrote... E. The maiden wrote... F. Jacob wrote... G. The
lad wrote... H. The family wrote...

Exercise 2 1. The family sent a lad. 2. Boaz walked.
3. Ruth remembered a gift. 4. The woman went. 5. The man
remembered a book. 6. She sent a man.

Exercise 3 1. הַנַּעַר 2. הַסֵּפֶר 3. הַמִּשְׁפָּחָה 4. הָאִישׁ 5. הַמִּנְחָה

6. הָאִשָּׁה 7. הַנַּעֲרָה

1. the lad 2. the book 3. the family 4. the man 5. the gift
6. the woman 7. the maiden

Exercise 4 1. כָּתַב 2. שָׁלְחָה 3. זָכַר 4. הָלְכָה 5. שָׁלַח

6. הָלַךְ 7. כָּתְבָה 8. זָכְרָה

3

Exercise 5   1. נַעַר כָּתַב סֵפֶר.   2. הַנַּעַר כָּתַב סֵפֶר.   3. נָעֳמִי
כָּתְבָה סֵפֶר.   4. הִיא כָּתְבָה סֵפֶר.   5. אִישׁ שָׁלַח מִנְחָה.   6. שָׁלַח הָאִישׁ
מִנְחָה.   7. הוּא שָׁלַח סֵפֶר.   8. בֹּעַז שָׁלַח נַעַר.   9. הַמִּשְׁפָּחָה שָׁלְחָה
מִנְחָה.   10. הָלַךְ אַבְרָהָם.

Exercise 6   1. הַמִּשְׁפָּחָה הָלְכָה.   2. דָּוִד זָכַר סֵפֶר.   3. הָאִשָּׁה שָׁלְחָה
מִנְחָה.   4. אַבְרָהָם שָׁלַח נַעַר.

1. The family walked. 2. David remembered a book. 3. The
woman sent a gift. 4. Abraham sent a young man.

Exercise 7   1. שָׂרָה שָׁלְחָה מִנְחָה.   2. יַעֲקֹב זָכַר סֵפֶר.   3. הוּא שָׁלַח
נַעֲרָה.   4. הָאִישׁ זָכַר מִשְׁפָּחָה.   5. הַנַּעַר כָּתַב סֵפֶר.   6. הִיא שָׁלְחָה
אִשָּׁה.

1. Sarah sent a gift. 2. Jacob remembered a book. 3. He
sent a young woman. 4. The man remembered a family. 5. The
young man wrote a book. 6. She sent a woman.

CHAPTER 6

Exercise 1   1. A. יַעֲקֹב וּבֹעַז הָלְכוּ וְזָכְרוּ.   B. שָׂרָה וְרוּת הָלְכוּ
וְזָכְרוּ.   C. הִיא הָלְכָה וְזָכְרָה.   D. הָאֲנָשִׁים הָלְכוּ וְזָכְרוּ.   E. הֵמָּה
הָלְכוּ וְזָכְרוּ.   F. הַנַּעֲרָה הָלְכָה וְזָכְרָה.   G. הַנָּשִׁים הָלְכוּ וְזָכְרוּ.
H. הוּא הָלַךְ וְזָכַר.   I. הֵנָּה הָלְכוּ וְזָכְרוּ.   J. הַנַּעַר הָלַךְ וְזָכַר.
2. A. הֵם שָׁלְחוּ סְפָרִים וּנְעָלִים.   B. הַנְּעָרוֹת שָׁלְחוּ...   C. הַמִּשְׁפָּחָה
שָׁלְחָה...   D. אַבְרָהָם שָׁלַח...   E. נָעֳמִי שָׁלְחָה...   F. הֵמָּה שָׁלְחוּ...
G. רוּת שָׁלְחָה...   H. יַעֲקֹב שָׁלַח...   I. הֵנָּה שָׁלְחוּ...   J. הַנְּעָרִים
שָׁלְחוּ...

1. Abraham walked and remembered. A. Jacob and Boaz walked
and remembered. B. Sarah and Ruth walked and remembered.
C. She walked and remembered. D. The men walked and remembered. E. They walked... F. The young woman walked...

G. The women walked... H. He walked... I. They walked...
J. The lad walked... 2. Sarah sent books and shoes.
A. They sent books and shoes. B. The maidens sent... C. The
family sent... D. Abraham sent... E. Naomi sent... F. They
sent... G. Ruth sent... H. Jacob sent... I. They sent...
J. The young men sent...

Exercise 2 ‎1. וְאִשָּׁה ‎2. וְאַבְרָהָם ‎3. וּמִשְׁפָּחָה ‎4. וִירוּשָׁלַ͏ַם

‎5. וְהִיא ‎6. וּבֹעַז ‎7. וְשָׂרָה ‎8. וּמִנְחָה ‎9. וְהַמִּשְׁפָּחָה ‎10. וְהַסֵּפֶר

Exercise 3 1. The woman wrote. 2. David wrote. 3. David
and the man walked. 4. The family went. 5. The men and the
women remembered houses. 6. The lads wrote a book. 7. The
maiden sent gifts. 8. Naomi remembered a road. 9. Ruth and
Boaz sent a pair of shoes. 10. Abraham remembered a woman.

Exercise 4 ‎1. כָּתַב ‎2. שָׁלְחוּ ‎3. זָכְרָה ‎4. הָלְכוּ ‎5. שָׁלְחָה

‎6. זָכְרוּ

Exercise 5 ‎1. הָאֲנָשִׁים שָׁלְחוּ נְעָרוֹת. ‎2. הַנְּעָרוֹת זָכְרוּ דְּרָכִים.

‎3. הֵם כָּתְבוּ סְפָרִים. ‎4. הַנָּשִׁים שָׁלְחוּ מְנָחוֹת.

Exercise 6 ‎1. הִיא כָּתְבָה סֵפֶר. ‎2. הָאִשָּׁה וְהָאִישׁ שָׁלְחוּ מִנְחָה.

‎3. הַנַּעֲרָה הָלְכָה וְזָכְרָה. ‎4. הוּא זָכַר דֶּרֶךְ.

Exercise 7 ‎1. הַנַּעַר וְהַנַּעֲרָה הָלְכוּ. ‎2. הָאֲנָשִׁים שָׁלְחוּ מְנָחוֹת.

‎3. הֵנָּה זָכְרוּ מִשְׁפָּחָה. ‎4. יַעֲקֹב וְאַבְרָהָם שָׁלְחוּ בַּעֲלִים. ‎5. הָאִישׁ

כָּתַב סְפָרִים. ‎6. הַמִּשְׁפָּחוֹת זָכְרוּ בַּיִת.

Exercise 8 ‎1. יַעֲקֹב וּבֹעַז הָלְכוּ. ‎2. רוּת וְהָאִשָּׁה שָׁלְחוּ מְנָחוֹת.

‎3. נָעֳמִי כָּתְבָה סְפָרִים. ‎4. הַנָּשִׁים זָכְרוּ.

1. Jacob and Boaz went. 2. Ruth and the woman sent gifts.
3. Naomi wrote books. 4. The women remembered.

CHAPTER 7

Exercise 1 ‎1. A. הַמִּשְׁפָּחָה שָׁלְחָה נַעַר מִבַּיִת לֶחֶם אֶל יְרוּשָׁלַ͏ַם.

‎B. הַנָּשִׁים שָׁלְחוּ נַעַר... ‎C. אֲנָשִׁים שָׁלְחוּ... ‎D. נָעֳמִי וּבֹעַז שָׁלְחוּ...

5

E. הֵנָּה שָׁלְחוּ. F... שָׂרָה שָׁלְחָה. G... אִשָּׁה שָׁלְחָה. 2. A. אַבְרָהָם

וְדָוִד הָלְכוּ לַבַּיִת. B. יַעֲקֹב הָלַךְ לַבַּיִת. C. הֵמָּה הָלְכוּ... D. רוּת

הָלְכָה... E. הוּא הָלַךְ... F. הֵנָּה הָלְכוּ... G. הִיא הָלְכָה...

3. A. הַמִּשְׁפָּחוֹת כָּתְבוּ עַל דָּוִד. B. הַנְּעָרִים כָּתְבוּ עַל דָּוִד. C. הָאִישׁ

כָּתַב... D. רוּת וְנָעֳמִי כָּתְבוּ... E. שָׂרָה וּבֹעַז כָּתְבוּ... F. הַנָּשִׁים

כָּתְבוּ... G. יַעֲקֹב כָּתַב... 4. A. הַנְּעָרוֹת הָלְכוּ כְּאַבְרָהָם. B. הוּא

הָלַךְ כְּאַבְרָהָם. C. הֵנָּה הָלְכוּ... D. הִיא הָלְכָה... E. הֵם הָלְכוּ...

F. הַנַּעַר וְהַנַּעֲרָה הָלְכוּ... G. יַעֲקֹב הָלַךְ...

1. The man sent a lad from Bethlehem to Jerusalem. A. The
family sent a lad from Bethlehem to Jerusalem. B. The women
sent a lad... C. The men sent... D. Naomi and Boaz sent...
E. They sent... F. Sarah sent... G. A woman sent... 2. The
lad and the maiden went to the house. A. Abraham and David
went to the house. B. Jacob went... C. They went... D. Ruth
went... E. He went... F. They went... G. She went... 3. Ruth
wrote about David. A. The families wrote about David. B. The
lads wrote... C. The man wrote... D. Ruth and Naomi wrote...
E. Sarah and Boaz wrote... F. The women wrote... G. Jacob
wrote... 4. The man walked like Abraham. A. The young women
walked like Abraham. B. He walked... C. They walked...
D. She walked... E. They walked... F. The lad and the
maiden walked... G. Jacob walked...

Exercise 2 1. אֶל הַבַּיִת. 2. בִּירוּשָׁלַם. 3. עִם הַנְּעָרוֹת. 4. מִן בֵּית

5. לֶחֶם עַל אַבְרָהָם. 6. אֶל הַבַּיִת. 7. בַּדֶּרֶךְ

1. Ruth walked to the house. 2. The man in Jerusalem wrote
a book. 3. The lads walked with the maidens to the road.
4. The families from Bethlehem sent gifts. 5. Sarah wrote
about Abraham. 6. The people sent women to the house.
7. David and Boaz remembered maidens on the road.

Exercise 3 1. בְּמִשְׁפָּחוֹת, כְּמִשְׁפָּחוֹת, לְמִשְׁפָּחוֹת. 2. בְּמִנְחָה, כְּמִנְחָה,

לְמִנְחָה. 3. בַּסֵּפֶר, כַּסֵּפֶר, לַסֵּפֶר. 4. בִּדְרָכִים, כִּדְרָכִים, לִדְרָכִים.

5. בַּבְּעָלִים, כַּבְּעָלִים, לַבְּעָלִים. 6. בָּאֲנָשִׁים, כָּאֲנָשִׁים, לָאֲנָשִׁים.

7. בִּירוּשָׁלַם, כִּירוּשָׁלַם, לִירוּשָׁלַם. 8. בַּבָּתִּים, כַּבָּתִּים, לַבָּתִּים.

1. with families, as, like families, to, for families   2. with

in a gift, as,like a gift, to,for a gift 3. in the book,
as,like the book, to,for the book 4. in,with roads, as,like
roads, to,for roads 5. with,in the pair of shoes, as,like
the pair of shoes, to,for the pair of shoes 6. with people,
as,like people, to,for people 7. in Jerusalem, as,like
Jerusalem, to,for Jerusalem 8. in the houses, as,like the
houses, to,for the houses

Exercise 4 1a. Boaz wrote a book. 1b. Boaz wrote to the
maiden. 1c. Boaz wrote to the maiden in Jerusalem. 1d. Boaz
wrote about the family to the maiden in Jerusalem. 1e. Ruth
and Boaz wrote about the family to the maiden in Jerusalem.
2a. Sarah walked to the road. 2b. Sarah walked from the
house to the road. 2c. Sarah and Jacob walked from the house
to the road. 2d. Sarah and Jacob walked with David from the
house to the road.

Exercise 5 1. הַמִּשְׁפָּחָה בְּבֵית לֶחֶם שָׁלְחָה מִנְחָה. 2. הַמִּשְׁפָּחָה בְּבֵית
לֶחֶם שָׁלְחָה מִנְחָה לְאִישׁ בִּירוּשָׁלַם. 3. הַמִּשְׁפָּחָה בְּבֵית לֶחֶם שָׁלְחָה מִנְחָה מִן
רוּת לְאִישׁ בִּירוּשָׁלַם. 4. הַמִּשְׁפָּחָה בְּבֵית לֶחֶם שָׁלְחָה נַעַר עִם מִנְחָה מִן
רוּת לְאִישׁ בִּירוּשָׁלַם. 5. הַמִּשְׁפָּחָה בְּבֵית לֶחֶם שָׁלְחָה נַעַר עִם סְפָרִים
כְּמִנְחָה לְאִישׁ בִּירוּשָׁלַם.

Exercise 6 1. דָּוִד זָכַר דֶּרֶךְ לִירוּשָׁלַם. 2. הֵנָּה כָּתְבוּ לַנָּשִׁים בְּבֵית
לֶחֶם. 3. הֵם שָׁלְחוּ בַּעֲרָה מִן הַבָּיִת. 4. נָעֳמִי הָלְכָה כְּאִשָּׁה.

Exercise 7 1. מִבֵּית לֶחֶם, אֶל יְרוּשָׁלַם 2. עִם בֹּעַז 3. לְאַבְרָהָם
4. כִּנְעָרוֹת, עַל הַנְּעָרִים 5. מִמּוֹאָב, אֶל יְהוּדָה 6. בִּירוּשָׁלַם

CHAPTER 8

Exercise 2 1. A. אַתָּה הָלַכְתָּ אֶל הַבָּיִת. B. אַתְּ הָלַכְתְּ אֶל הַבָּיִת.
C. הוּא הָלַךְ... D. הִיא הָלְכָה. E. אֲנַחְנוּ הָלַכְנוּ... F. אַתֶּם הֲלַכְתֶּם
... G. אַתֶּן הֲלַכְתֶּן. H. הֵם הָלְכוּ. I. הֵנָּה הָלְכוּ... 2. A. הֵם
שָׁלְחוּ בְּעָלַים אֶל הַנָּשִׁים. B. אַתְּ שָׁלַחַתְּ בְּעָלַים אֶל הַנָּשִׁים. C. אֲנַחְנוּ
שָׁלַחְנוּ בְּעָלַים אֶל הַנָּשִׁים. D. אַתֶּן שְׁלַחְתֶּן... E. הִיא שָׁלְחָה...
F. אַתָּה שָׁלַחְתָּ... G. הֵנָּה שָׁלְחוּ... H. אֲנִי שָׁלַחְתִּי... I. הֵמָּה שָׁלְחוּ...

J. אָנֹכִי שָׁלַחְתִּי... 3. A. אַתֶּם זְכַרְתֶּם אִישׁ מִבֵּית לֶחֶם. B. אֲנַחְנוּ
זָכַרְנוּ... C. הוּא זָכַר... D. הֵם זָכְרוּ... E. אַתָּה זָכַרְתָּ... F. הֵנָּה
זָכְרוּ... G. אֲנִי זָכַרְתִּי... H. אַתֶּן זְכַרְתֶּן...

1. I went to the house. A. You went to the house. B. You
went to the house. C. He went... D. She went... E. We went...
F. You went... G. You went... H. They went... I. They went..
2. He sent a pair of shoes to the women. A. They sent a pair
of shoes to the women. B. You sent... C. We sent... D. You
sent... E. She sent... F. You sent... G. They sent... H. I
sent... I. They sent... J. I sent... 3. You remembered a
man from Bethlehem. A. You remembered a man from Bethlehem.
B. We remembered... C. He remembered... D. They remembered...
E. You remembered... F. They remembered... G. I remembered...
H. You remembered...

Exercise 3a 1. הָלַכְנוּ מִן הַדֶּרֶךְ אֶל הַבָּיִת. 2. הֵנָּה שָׁלְחוּ נַעַר אֶל
בֹּעַז. 3. כְּתַבְתֶּם סֵפֶר עַל מוֹאָב. 4. הֵם זָכְרוּ נַעֲרָה. 5. כְּתַבְתֶּן
אֶל הַנָּשִׁים וְאֶל הָאֲנָשִׁים מִבֵּית לֶחֶם. 6. הֵמָּה שָׁלְחוּ סְפָרִים לְרוּת.

Exercise 3b 1. כְּתַבְתָּ עַל בֹּעַז וְעַל בָּעֳמִי. 2. הִיא שָׁלְחָה בַּעֲלַיִם אֶל
הַנַּעַר מִן מוֹאָב. 3. זָכַרְתְּ דֶּרֶךְ אֶל הַבָּיִת. 4. הָלַכְתִּי עִם הָאֲנָשִׁים
מִירוּשָׁלַ͏ִם. 5. הוּא כָּתַב אֶל הַנָּשִׁים עַל בֵּית לֶחֶם. 6. זָכַרְתִּי אִישׁ כְּבֹעַז.

Exercise 4 1. הָלַכְתִּי 2. שָׁלְחָה 3. זְכַרְתֶּם 4. כָּתְבָה 5. הָלַכְנוּ
6. שָׁלְחוּ 7. זָכַר 8. כָּתַבְתְּ 9. הָלְכוּ 10. שְׁלַחְתֶּן

Exercise 5 1. אֲנַחְנוּ שָׁלַחְנוּ בַּעֲלַיִם. 2. אַתֶּם זְכַרְתֶּם אִישׁ. 3. אַתֶּן
כְּתַבְתֶּן אֶל דָּוִד. 4. הֵנָּה הָלְכוּ אֶל הַבָּיִת. 5. הֵמָּה שָׁלְחוּ מִנְחָה.
6. הֵם זָכְרוּ נְעָרִים מִמּוֹאָב.

Exercise 6 1. שָׁלַחְנוּ בַּעֲלַיִם מִמּוֹאָב. 2. שָׁלַחְתְּ סְפָרִים לְמִשְׁפָּחָה.
3. זָכַרְתִּי אִישׁ וְאִשָּׁה. 4. כְּתַבְתֶּם לְאִשָּׁה עַל הַמִּנְחָה. 5. הֵם הָלְכוּ עִם
שָׂרָה וְיַעֲקֹב לִירוּשָׁלַ͏ִם.

Exercise 7 1. הֵם כָּתְבוּ עַל הָאִישׁ. 2. אַתֶּם זְכַרְתֶּם סְפָרִים.
3. הִיא הָלְכָה אֶל הַבָּיִת. 4. שָׁלַחְתְּ מִנְחָה עִם אַבְרָהָם.

8

1. They wrote about the man.   2. You remembered books.   3. She went to the house.   4. You sent a present with Abraham.

CHAPTER 9

Exercise 1   A. בֹּעַז שָׁלַח אֶת הַסֵּפֶר אֶל מוֹאָב.   B. בֹּעַז שָׁלַח
נְעָלִים אֶל מוֹאָב...   C. בֹּעַז שָׁלַח אֶת רוּת...   D. בֹּעַז שָׁלַח אֶת הַנְּעָרִים...
E. בֹּעַז שָׁלַח בַּת...   F. בֹּעַז שָׁלַח אֶת נָעֳמִי...   G. בֹּעַז שָׁלַח אֶת הַבָּנִים
H... בֹּעַז שָׁלַח אֲנָשִׁים...   I. בֹּעַז שָׁלַח דָּבָר...   2. A. הִיא הָלְכָה אֶל
עִיר.   B... אֶל הַבֵּן.   C... אֶל בֵּית לֶחֶם.   D... אֶל הַדֶּרֶךְ.
E... אֶל יְהוּדָה.   F... אֶל נַעַר.   G... אֶל הַבָּנוֹת.   H... אֶל
הַשָּׂדֶה.   3. A. הַנַּעַר זָכַר אֶת הַדְּבָרִים בָּאָרֶץ.   B... זָכַרְתִּי.   C. זָכַרְתָּ
D... .   E. הֵנָּה זָכְרוּ...   F... זְכַרְתֶּם.   G. זָכַרְתְּ...
H. זָכַרְנוּ...   I. זְכַרְתֶּן...   4. A. כָּתַבְתִּי אֶת הַסֵּפֶר וְלֹא שָׁלַחְתִּי אֶת
הַסֵּפֶר לְרוּת.   B. כָּתַבְתְּ אֶת הַסֵּפֶר וְלֹא שָׁלַחְתְּ...   C. הִיא כָּתְבָה...
D. כָּתַבְנוּ...וְלֹא שָׁלַחְנוּ...   E. כָּתַבְתָּ...וְלֹא שָׁלַחְתָּ...
F. כְּתַבְתֶּם...וְלֹא שְׁלַחְתֶּם...   G. הֵנָּה כָּתְבוּ...וְלֹא שָׁלְחוּ...   H. כָּתַבְתִּי...
וְלֹא שָׁלַחְתִּי...   I. הֵמָּה כָּתְבוּ...וְלֹא שָׁלְחוּ...

1. Boaz sent the maidens to Moab. A. Boaz sent the book to Moab. B. Boaz sent shoes to Moab. C. Boaz sent Ruth... D. Boaz sent the young men... E. Boaz sent a daughter... F. Boaz sent Naomi... G. Boaz sent the sons... H. Boaz sent people... I. Boaz sent a thing... 2. She went to the house. A. She went to a city. B. She went to the son. C. ...to Bethlehem. D. ...to the road. E. ...to Judah. F. ...to a lad. G. ...to the daughters. H. ...to the field. 3. The daughter remembered the things in the land. A. The lad remembered the things in the land. B. I remembered... C. You remembered... D. They remembered... E. They remembered... F. You remembered... G. You remembered... H. We remembered.. I. You remembered... 4. He wrote the book and he did not send the book to Ruth. A. I wrote the book and I did not send the book to Ruth. B. You wrote the book and you did not send... C. She wrote...and she did not send... D. We wrote.. and we did not send... E. You wrote...and you did not send.. F. You wrote...and you did not send... G. They wrote...and

they did not send... H. You wrote...and you did not send...
I. They wrote...and they did not send...

Exercise 2 .1 הִיא כָּתְבָה אֶת הַסְּפָרִים. 2. הָאִישׁ שָׁלַח אֶת הַנַּעֲרָה אֶל

בֵּית לֶחֶם. 3. רוּת וְאַבְרָהָם זָכְרוּ אֶת הַדֶּרֶךְ. 4. שָׁלַחְתְּ אֶת הַנַּעֲלַיִם

לְרוּת. 5. הוּא זָכַר אֶת הַשּׁוֹפֵט מִן הָאָרֶץ. 6. זְכַרְתֶּם אֶת הָאִשָּׁה מִן

הַבַּיִת. 7. הַיּוֹם זָכַרְתִּי אֶת הַשָּׂדוֹת בְּמוֹאָב.

Exercise 3 .1-- .2-- .3-- .4-- .5 אֶת הַנַּעַר וְאֶת הַנַּעֲרָה.

1. Boaz sent a lad to the field. 2. Ruth wrote a book about
Judah. 3. The man sent the family to Moab. 4. The son
remembered a road and a city. 5. Naomi sent the lad and the
maiden.

Exercise 4 .1a רוּת הָלְכָה לָעִיר. 1b. רוּת הָלְכָה לָעִיר. 1c. רוּת

הָלְכָה בְּעִיר. 1d. רוּת הָלְכָה בָּעִיר. 1e. רוּת לֹא הָלְכָה בָּעִיר.

1f. לֹא רוּת הָלְכָה בָּעִיר. 1g. לֹא בָּעִיר הָלְכָה רוּת. 2a. בֹּעַז כָּתַב

סֵפֶר עַל בָּתִּים. 2b. בֹּעַז כָּתַב אֶת הַסֵּפֶר עַל בָּתִּים. 2c. בֹּעַז לֹא כָּתַב

אֶת הַסֵּפֶר עַל בָּתִּים. 2d. לֹא בֹּעַז כָּתַב אֶת הַסֵּפֶר עַל בָּתִּים. 2e. לֹא עַל

בָּתִּים כָּתַב בֹּעַז.

Exercise 5 .1 רוּת וְנָעֳמִי הָלְכוּ מִן הָעִיר. 2. רוּת כָּתְבָה לַבָּנִים

וְלַבָּנוֹת. 3. הָאִישׁ זָכַר אֶת הַדָּבָר. 4. יַעֲקֹב הָלַךְ אֶל הָעִיר. 5. הִיא

זָכְרָה אֶת בֵּית לֶחֶם.

1. Ruth and Naomi went from the city. 2. Ruth wrote to the
sons and to the daughters. 3. The man remembered the word.
4. Jacob walked to the city. 5. She remembered Bethlehem.

Exercise 6 .1 רוּת וְנָעֳמִי לֹא הָלְכוּ... 2. רוּת לֹא כָּתְבָה...

3. הָאִישׁ לֹא זָכַר... 4. יַעֲקֹב לֹא הָלַךְ... 5. הִיא לֹא זָכְרָה...

Exercise 7 1. The son remembered the woman and the lad
today. 2. He sent a pair of shoes and a book to the maidens.
3. They did not go with Naomi and Ruth from the house to the
road today. 4. The judge, and not David, wrote the words.
5. The woman remembered the days in Jerusalem.

10

Exercise 8 1. הָאִישׁ, הַנַּעַר = definite direct object 2. נְעָלִים

, סֵפֶר = indefinite direct object, הַנְּעָרוֹת = object of prep

3. נָעֳמִי, רוּת, הַבַּיִת, הַדֶּרֶךְ = object of preposition

4. הַדְּבָרִים = definite direct object

5. הַיָּמִים = definite direct object, יְרוּשָׁלַם = object of prep.

Exercise 9. We remembered the days in Bethlehem. I remembered the city and the fields. You remembered the people and the families. Abraham and Boaz did not remember the city and they did not remember the people; they remembered the judge.

CHAPTER 10

Exercise 2 1. הָיִיתִי עִם הַשֹּׁפֵט. B. רוּת הָיְתָה עִם הַשֹּׁפֵט.

C. הָיִיתָ ... D. בֹּעַז וְנָעֳמִי הָיוּ ... E. הָיִינוּ ....

F. הַנְּעָרִים הָיוּ ... G. הֱיִיתֶן ... H. הָיִיתָ .... I. הֱיִיתֶם...

... J. הַבֵּן הָיָה ... 2. A. שָׁמַרְנוּ אֶת הָאֹכֶל כִּי הָיָה רָעָב בָּעִיר.

B. שָׁמַרְתָּ אֶת הָאֹכֶל כִּי הָיָה רָעָב בָּעִיר. C. הֵנָּה שָׁמְרוּ אֶת הָאֹכֶל כִּי הָיָה

רָעָב בָּעִיר. D. הִיא שָׁמְרָה ... E. הָאֲנָשִׁים שָׁמְרוּ ... F. שְׁמַרְתֶּן...

G. שָׁמַרְתִּי ... H. שְׁמַרְתֶּם ... 3. A. אָמַרְתָּ: " הַמִּנְחָה הָיְתָה בַּבַּיִת."

B. רוּת אָמְרָה: "הַמִּנְחָה הָיְתָה בַּבַּיִת." C. אָמַרְנוּ ... D. הֵנָּה אָמְרוּ...

E. הוּא אָמַר ... F. הֵם אָמְרוּ ... G. אָמַרְתִּי ... H. אָמַרְתְּ...

4. A. אַבְרָהָם אֲשֶׁר הָיָה מִמּוֹאָב אָכַל אֶת הַלֶּחֶם הַיּוֹם. B. אֲנִי אֲשֶׁר

הָיִיתִי מִמּוֹאָב אָכַלְתִּי ... C. אַתֶּן אֲשֶׁר הֱיִיתֶן מִמּוֹאָב אֲכַלְתֶּן. D. אַתְּ

אֲשֶׁר הָיִית מִמּוֹאָב אָכַלְתְּ ... E. אֲנַחְנוּ אֲשֶׁר הָיִינוּ מִמּוֹאָב אָכַלְנוּ ...

F. הֵמָּה אֲשֶׁר הָיוּ מִמּוֹאָב אָכְלוּ ... G. אַתָּה אֲשֶׁר הָיִיתָ מִמּוֹאָב אָכַלְתָּ...

H. הַבָּנוֹת אֲשֶׁר הָיוּ מִמּוֹאָב אָכְלוּ ...

1. The man was with the judge. A. I was with the judge.
B. Ruth was with the judge. C. You were... D. Boaz and Naomi
were... E. We were... F. The lads were... G. You were...

H. You were... I. You were... J. The son was... 2. The judge
guarded the food because there was a famine in the city.
A. We guarded the food because there was a famine in the
city. B. You guarded... C. They guarded... D. She guarded...
E. The people guarded... F. You guarded... G. I guarded...
H. You guarded... 3. The women said: "The gift was in the
house." A. You said: "The gift was in the house." B. Ruth
said... C. We said... D. They said... E. He said... F. They
said... G. I said... H. You said... 4. The family that was
from Moab ate the bread today. A. Abraham, who was from
Moab, ate the bread today. B. I, who was from Moab, ate...
C. You, who were from Moab, ate... D. You, who were from
Moab, ate... E. We, who were from Moab, ate... F. They, who
were from Moab, ate... G. You, who were from Moab, ate...
H. The daughters who were from Moab ate...

3 m or f,pl .3 הִיא - 3 f sg .2 אַתֵּן - 2 f pl .1 Exercise 3

3 m sg .6 אַתָּ - 2 f sg .5 אָנֹכִי or אֲנִי - 1 c sg .4 הֵמָּה, הֵנָּה -

אֲנִי or אָנֹכִי - 1 c sg .9 אַתֶּם - 2 m pl .8 אַתָּה - 2 m sg .7 הוּא

- 2 f pl .12 הֵם, הֵנָּה - 3,m or f,pl .11 הִיא - 3 f sg .10

- 3,m or f,pl .15 אַתֶּם - 2 m pl .14 אֲנַחְנוּ - 1 c pl .13 אַתֵּן

הֵמָּה, הֵנָּה .16 1 c pl - אֲנַחְנוּ

פָּתְבוּ .5 הָיָה, הָיְתָה .4 שָׁמְרָה .3 הָיִינוּ .2 הָלַךְ .1 Exercise 4

הָיִיתִי .11 זָכַר .10 הָיוּ .9 אֲכַלְתֶּם .8 שָׁמַרְתָּ .7 הֱיִיתֶם .6

שָׁמַרְתִּי .14 אָמַר .13 אֲכַלְתֶּן .12 הָיְתָה

1. The judge went from Bethlehem to Moab. 2. We were in the
fields. 3. She guarded the road two days. 4. Abraham was a
son and Naomi was a daughter. 5. Boaz and David wrote about
the food. 6. You were with the judges there. 7. You did not
guard the shoes. 8. You ate with the family. 9. They were
with the women. 10. The young man remembered the things in
Jerusalem. 11. I was not with Ruth in the field because Ruth
was in Bethlehem. 12. You ate with David there. 13. Jacob
said to the man: "Not today." 14. I did not guard the thing.

Exercise 5 1. There were no people in the land because
there was a famine there. 2. We wrote to Jacob that Abraham
was in Jerusalem. 3. David was the man that guarded the
cities. 4. Abraham wrote to Boaz because Boaz was a judge.
5. The young woman who was in the house went to the field.
6. The sons ate in the city because there was bread there.
7. Sarah remembered the lad who went to Bethlehem. 8. The

man sent books to the daughter in Jerusalem because there
were no books there. 9. The man was like a son to Abraham
because he guarded the house.

CHAPTER 11

Exercise 1 .1 A. יָשַׁבְנוּ בְּאֶרֶץ טוֹבָה. B. הַמֶּלֶךְ יָשַׁב בְּאֶרֶץ טוֹבָה.
C. הֵנָּה יָשְׁבוּ בְּאֶרֶץ טוֹבָה. D. יָשַׁבְתָּ... E. אַתָּה וְדָוִד וְיָשַׁבְתֶּם...
F. יַעֲקֹב וְאַבְרָהָם יָשְׁבוּ... G. ...יָשַׁבְתְּ... 2. A. הָאֵם הַטּוֹבָה הָלְכָה אֶל
הָעִיר. B. הַנְּעָרוֹת הַטּוֹבוֹת הָלְכוּ... C. הָאָב הַטּוֹב הָלַךְ... D. הַבָּנִים
הַטּוֹבִים הָלְכוּ... E. הַבַּת הַטּוֹבָה הָלְכָה... 3. A. הַשֹּׁפֵט הַזָּקֵן בַּשָּׂדֶה
הַגָּדוֹל הַיּוֹם. B. הַשֹּׁפֵט הַזָּקֵן בָּעִיר הַגְּדוֹלָה הַיּוֹם. C. הַשֹּׁפֵט הַזָּקֵן
בַּשָּׂדוֹת הַגְּדוֹלִים... D. הַשֹּׁפֵט הַזָּקֵן בַּדְּרָכִים הַגְּדוֹלוֹת... 4. A. הָאִשָּׁה
מִמּוֹאָב אִשָּׁה קְדוֹשָׁה. B. הָאִמּוֹת מִמּוֹאָב נָשִׁים קְדוֹשׁוֹת. C. הַשּׁוֹפֵט מִמּוֹאָב
אִישׁ קָדוֹשׁ. D. הַמְּלָכִים מִמּוֹאָב אֲנָשִׁים קְדוֹשִׁים. E. הַבָּנוֹת מִמּוֹאָב נָשִׁים
קְדוֹשׁוֹת. 5. A. הָיִינוּ אֲנָשִׁים רָעִים. B. רוּת וְנָעֳמִי הָיוּ נָשִׁים רָעוֹת.
C. הֵמָּה הָיוּ אֲנָשִׁים רָעִים. D. הֱיִיתֶן נָשִׁים רָעוֹת. E. הִיא הָיְתָה אִשָּׁה
רָעָה. F. הָיִיתִי אִשָּׁה רָעָה. G. הָיִיתָ אִישׁ רַע. H. הֱיִיתֶם אֲנָשִׁים רָעִים.
I. הָיִיתְ אִשָּׁה רָעָה.

1. She settled in a good land. A. We settled in a good land.
B. The king settled in a good land. C. They settled... D. You
settled... E. You and David settled... F. Jacob and Abraham
settled... G. You settled... 2. The good man went to the
city. A. The good mother went to the city. B. The good
maidens went... C. The good father went... D. The good sons
went... E. The good daughter went... 3. The old judge is in
the big house today. A. The old judge is in the big field
today. B. ...is in the big city... C. ...in the big fields...
D. ...on the big roads... 4. The fathers from Moab are holy
men. A. The woman from Moab is a holy woman. B. The mothers
from Moab are holy women. C. The judge from Moab is a holy
man. D. The kings from Moab are holy men. E. The daughters
from Moab are holy women. 5. The king was an evil man.
A. We were evil people. B. Ruth and Naomi were evil women.
C. They were evil men. D. You were evil women. E. She was an

13

evil woman. F. I was an evil woman. G. You were an evil man.
H. You were evil men. I. You were an evil woman.

Exercise 2   1. קָדוֹשׁ   2. זְקֵנוֹת   3. רָעִים   4. גְּדוֹלָה   5. טוֹבוֹת

6. קְדוֹשָׁה   7. גְּדוֹלִים   8. הַטּוֹבִים   9. אֶחָד   10. טוֹבִים   11. זָקֵן

Exercise 3   1a. an old man or A man is old.   2a. The man
is old.   3a. the old man   1b. a good gift or A gift is
good.   2b. The gift is good.   3b. the good gift   1c. great
kings or Kings are great.   2c. The kings are great.
3c. The great kings are evil.

Exercise 4   1. רוּת הָיְתָה בְּעֵרָה וּבְעָמִי הָיְתָה אִשָּׁה.   2. הַמֶּלֶךְ

וְהַשֹּׁפְטִים הָיוּ בַּדֶּרֶךְ הָאַחַת לְמוֹאָב.   3. הָיִינוּ בַּבַּיִת וְהֵם הָיוּ בַּשָּׂדֶה.

4. הִיא הָיְתָה עִם הַנָּשִׁים כִּי אַתֶּם הֱיִיתֶם עִם הַמֶּלֶךְ.   5. הַלֶּחֶם הַטּוֹב הָיָה

בַּבַּיִת.   6. הָיִית פְּאֵם לְרוּת.   7. הָיִיתָ אָב לְיַעֲקֹב.   8. שָׂרָה הָיְתָה

בְּעֵרָה מִיהוּדָה.   9. שׁוֹפֵט אֶחָד הָיָה בַּשָּׂדֶה עִם דָּוִד.

Exercise 5   1. אֲנַחְנוּ עִם אַבְרָהָם בַּדֶּרֶךְ לְמוֹאָב.   2. הַדְּבָרִים מֵעִיר

יְהוּדָה.   3. אַתָּה בְּמוֹאָב כִּי לֶחֶם בַּשָּׂדוֹת שָׁם.   4. אַתֶּן עִם הַנָּשִׁים

הַטּוֹבוֹת בִּירוּשָׁלַםִ.   5. אַתְּ אֵם לְיַעֲקֹב וּבַת לְאַבְרָהָם.   6. דָּוִד בַּבַּיִת

הַגָּדוֹל.   7. אִשָּׁה אַחַת בַּשָּׂדֶה.

Exercise 7   There was a family that settled in Judah. The
old mother was Sarah and the old father was Boaz. The
daughter in the family, Ruth, was good and the son, Jacob,
was bad. There was a great famine in Judah and there was no
bread. Sarah and Boaz sent Ruth and Jacob to Moab because
there was food there. When Ruth was in Moab, she remembered
the family and she sent food to the family and to the people
in Judah. The evil Jacob did not remember the father and the
mother and did not send food to Judah. When there was bread
in Judah, Ruth went from Moab to the family in Judah. The
evil Jacob stayed in Moab.

2. זְקֵנָה, זָקֵן, טוֹבָה, רַע, גָּדוֹל   3. הָאֵם הַזְּקֵנָה שָׂרָה וְהָאָב הַזָּקֵן

בֹּעַז.   4. אֶת רוּת וְאֶת יַעֲקֹב, רַע.   4. אֶת רוּת וְאֶת יַעֲקֹב, אֶת הַמִּשְׁפָּחָה, אֶת

הָאָב וְאֶת הָאֵם   5. אֹכֶל

14

CHAPTER 12

Exercise 1   1. A. שׁוֹפֵט הַמָּקוֹם שָׁמַר אֶת שְׂדֵה הָאִשָּׁה הַזְּקֵנָה מְאֹד.
B. נַעֲרֵי הַמָּקוֹם שָׁמְרוּ... C. מֶלֶךְ הַמָּקוֹם שָׁמַר... D. נַעֲרוֹת הַמָּקוֹם שָׁמְרוּ... E. נַעֲרַת הַמָּקוֹם שָׁמְרָה... 2. A. כָּל הַלַּיְלָה הָיִינוּ בְּבֵית הָאֵם. B. כָּל הַלַּיְלָה בַּת הַמִּשְׁפָּחָה הָיְתָה בְּבֵית הָאֵם. C. כָּל הַלַּיְלָה הָיִיתִי... D. ...הֵמָּה הָיוּ... E. ...הָיִיתָ... F. ...הָיִית... G. ...הֱיִיתֶן... H. ...הֵנָּה הָיוּ... 3. A. אִם יַעֲקֹב הַזָּקֵן אָכְלָה עִם מִשְׁפַּחַת רוּת כָּל בֹּקֶר. B. אִם יַעֲקֹב הַטּוֹב אָכְלָה... C. אִם יַעֲקֹב הָרָעָה אָכְלָה. D. אִם יַעֲקֹב הַגָּדוֹל... E. אִם יַעֲקֹב הַקְּדוֹשָׁה אָכְלָה... 4. A. נַעֲרוֹת הָעִיר עוֹד זָכְרוּ אֶת יְמֵי דָוִד הַמֶּלֶךְ. B. עוֹד זָכַרְתִּי אֶת יְמֵי דָוִד הַמֶּלֶךְ. C. עוֹד זְכַרְתֶּם... D. עוֹד זָכַרְתָּ... E. עַם יִשְׂרָאֵל עוֹד זָכַר... F. עוֹד זָכַרְנוּ... G. עוֹד זָכַרְתְּ... H. בַּת הַשֹּׁפֵט עוֹד זָכְרָה... 5. A. ...כָּתַבְנוּ כִּי רַע הָאִישׁ הַזָּקֵן מִבַּעַז. B. כָּל נְשֵׁי הַמָּקוֹם כָּתְבוּ כִּי... C. ...כָּתַבְתָּ. D. ...כְּתַבְתֶּן. E. ...כָּתַבְתִּי. F. ...שׁוֹפְטֵי יְהוּדָה כָּתְבוּ... G. ...אֵשֶׁת יַעֲקֹב כָּתְבָה. H. ...כְּתַבְתֶּם. I. ...בֶּן אַבְרָהָם כָּתַב... 6. A. בַּבֹּקֶר לֹא הָלַכְתִּי וְלֹא יָשַׁבְתִּי כְּאִישׁ זָקֵן. B. בַּבֹּקֶר לֹא הָלַכְתְּ וְלֹא יָשַׁבְתְּ כְּאִשָּׁה זְקֵנָה. C. בַּבֹּקֶר אִם שָׂרָה לֹא הָלְכָה וְלֹא יָשְׁבָה כְּאִשָּׁה זְקֵנָה. D. בַּבֹּקֶר נַעַר הַשָּׂדֶה לֹא הָלַךְ וְלֹא יָשַׁב כְּאִישׁ זָקֵן. E. בַּבֹּקֶר לֹא הֲלַכְתֶּם וְלֹא יְשַׁבְתֶּם כַּאֲנָשִׁים זְקֵנִים.

1. The people of the place guarded the very old woman's field.
A. The judge of the place guarded the very old woman's field.
B. The lads of the place guarded...C. The king of the place
guarded...D. The young women of the place guarded...E. The
maiden of the place guarded...2. All night, the son was in the
mother's house. A. All night, we were in the mother's house.
B. All night, the daughter of the family was... C.All night, I
was...D. All night, they were...E...you were...F...you were...
G. ...you were... H. ...they were... 3. Jacob's old mother
ate with Ruth's family every morning. A. Old Jacob's mother
ate with Ruth's family every morning. B. Good Jacob's mother
ate... C. Jacob's evil mother ate... D. Big Jacob's mother

ate... E. Jacob's holy mother ate... 4. The people of Judah still remembered the days of King David. A. The maidens of the city still remembered the days of King David. B. I still remembered... C. You still remembered... D. You still remembered... E. The nation of Israel still remembered... F. We still remembered... G. You still remembered... H. The judge's daughter still remembered... 5. You wrote that the old man is more evil than Boaz. A. We wrote that the old man is more evil than Boaz. B. All the women of the place wrote.. C. You wrote... D. You wrote... E. I wrote... F. The judges of Judah wrote... G. Jacob's wife wrote... H. You wrote... I. Abraham's son wrote... 6. In the morning, he did not walk and did not sit like an old man. A. In the morning, I did not walk and did not sit like an old man. B. In the morning, you did not walk and did not sit like an old woman. C. In the morning, Sarah's mother did not walk and did not sit like an old woman. D. In the morning, the lad of the field did not walk and did not sit like an old man. E. In the morning, you did not walk and did not sit like old men.

Exercise 2 1. בֵּית מֶלֶךְ 2. חֶסֶד מְלָכִים 3. עִיר דָּוִד 4. בֶּן שׁוֹפֵט

5. אֵם נְעָרוֹת 6. שׁוֹפֵט אֲנָשִׁים 7. שׁוֹפֵט אִישׁ 8. אֹכֶל שָׂרָה 9. בַּת

אִשָּׁה 10. בָּתֵּי אֲנָשִׁים 11. דִּבְרֵי שׁוֹפְטִים 12. אַנְשֵׁי מָקוֹם

13. מִשְׁפְּחוֹת עָרִים 14. עֵינֵי אַבְרָהָם 15. אֲבוֹת נְעָרִים 16. יְדֵי בֹּעַז

17. חַסְדֵי אָבוֹת 18. מְקוֹם הַנְּעָרוֹת 19. יַד הַנַּעַר 20. סִפְרֵי הַשּׁוֹפְטִים

21. דִּבְרֵי הָאָבוֹת 22. נַעֲלֵי הָאִשָּׁה 23. חַסְדֵי הַמֶּלֶךְ 24. בְּנֵי הָעָם

25. דַּרְכֵי הָאָרֶץ

1. a king's house 2. kindness of kings 3. David's city 4. a son of a judge 5. a mother of maidens 6. a judge of men 7. a man's judge 8. Sarah's food 9. a woman's daughter 10. peoples' houses 11. words of judges 12. people of a place 13. families of cities 14. Abraham's eyes 15. fathers of lads 16. Boaz's hands 17. kindnesses of fathers 18. the place of the maidens 19. the lad's hand 20. the books of the judges 21. the words of the fathers 22. the woman's pair of shoes 23. the king's kindnesses 24. the sons of the nation 25. the roads of the land

Exercise 3 1. the gifts of the women - the women's gifts 2. the cities of Judah 3. days of famine 4. the house of the mother - the mother's house 5. the father of the lad - the lad's father 6. the son of the king - the king's son 7. the wife of Abraham - Abraham's wife 8. the nation of Israel 9. the people of the place

Exercise 4 1. מְנָחוֹת/הַנָּשִׁים 2. עָרִים/יְהוּדָה 3. יָמִים/רָעָב

4. בַּיִת/הָאֵם 5. אָב/הַנַּעַר 6. בֶּן/הַמֶּלֶךְ 7. אִשָּׁה/אַבְרָהָם 8. עַם/

9. אֲנָשִׁים/הַמָּקוֹם יִשְׂרָאֵל

Exercise 5 1. the man's son 2. the good man's son - the
man's good son 3. The man's son is good. 4. The good man's
son is in the city. - The man's good son is in the city.
5. The good man's sons are in the big city. 6. The man's
good sons are in the big city. 7. The sons of the good men
are in the big city today. - The men's good sons are in the
big city today. 8. The sons of the good people are good.

Exercise 6 1. מִשְׁפַּחַת מֶלֶךְ 2. מִשְׁפַּחַת הַמֶּלֶךְ 3. מִשְׁפַּחַת הַמֶּלֶךְ הַגָּדוֹל

4. מִשְׁפַּחַת הַמֶּלֶךְ הַגְּדוֹלָה 5. מִשְׁפַּחַת הַמֶּלֶךְ גְּדוֹלָה. 6. מִשְׁפַּחַת הַמֶּלֶךְ

הַגְּדוֹלָה לֹא בַּשָּׂדֶה. 7. מִשְׁפַּחַת הַמֶּלֶךְ הַגָּדוֹל גְּדוֹלָה. 8. אַנְשֵׁי מָקוֹם

9. אַנְשֵׁי הַמָּקוֹם 10. אַנְשֵׁי הַמָּקוֹם הָרָעִים 11. אַנְשֵׁי הַמָּקוֹם הָרַע

12. אַנְשֵׁי הַמָּקוֹם רָעִים. 13. אַנְשֵׁי הַמָּקוֹם הָרַע רָעִים. 14. אַנְשֵׁי

הַמָּקוֹם הָרַע לֹא טוֹבִים.

Exercise 7 1. The place is very good in Ruth's eyes.
2. Holy places were in the hands of the people of Judah.
3. A very great nation still stayed in the land of Israel.
4. The food was still in the house because the men were
still in the field. 5. Every morning, Boaz's lads ate bread
in a good place. 6. At night, all the maidens of the king
went to the women's house. 7. In the morning, Ruth said "No"
and at night, Ruth still said "No". 8. All the king's gifts
were in the hands of the men of the city. 9. I wrote about
the kindnesses of the judge to Ruth. 10. David's wife walked
on the road to Bethlehem the whole night. 11. Naomi's eyes
were very big.

Construct Units: 1. בְּעֵינֵי רוּת 2. בְּיָדֵי עַם יְהוּדָה 3. בְּאֶרֶץ

יִשְׂרָאֵל 5. נַעֲרֵי בֹּעַז 6. נַעֲרוֹת הַמֶּלֶךְ, בֵּית הַנָּשִׁים 8. מְנָחוֹת הַמֶּלֶךְ,

בְּיָדֵי אַנְשֵׁי הָעִיר 9. חַסְדֵי הַשׁוֹפֵט 10. אֵשֶׁת דָּוִד 11. עֵינֵי נָעֳמִי

CHAPTER 13

Exercise 2 1. A. מִי בְּבֵיתְךָ עִם בְּנֶךָ? B. מִי בְּבֵיתוֹ עִם בְּנוֹ?

17

‎C. מִי בְּבֵיתֵנוּ עִם בְּנֵנוּ? D. מִי בְּבֵיתְכֶם עִם בְּנְכֶם? E. מִי בְּבֵיתָהּ עִם

‎בְּנָהּ? F. מִי בְּבֵיתְךָ עִם בְּנְךָ? G. מִי בְּבֵיתָהּ עִם בְּנָהּ? H. מִי בְּבֵיתָן

‎עִם בְּנָן? I. מִי בְּבֵיתָם עִם בְּנָם? 2. A. מַה בְּיָדָם? סְפְרָם בְּיָדָם. B. מַה

‎בְּיָדֵה? סִפְרָהּ בְּיָדָהּ. C. ...בְּיָדֵנוּ? סְפְרֵנוּ... D. ...בְּיָדְךָ? סִפְרְךָ...

‎E. ...בְּיָדְכֶם? סִפְרְכֶם? F. ...בְּיָדוֹ? סְפְרוֹ... G. ...בְּיָדֵךְ? סִפְרֵךְ...

‎H. ...בְּיָדָהּ? סְפָרָהּ... I. ...בְּיָדְכֶן? סִפְרְכֶן... 3. A. לֹא זָכַרְתִּי אֶת

‎בְּנָהּ הַטּוֹב. B. ...אִמּוֹ הַטּוֹבָה. C. ...הַמֶּלֶךְ הַטּוֹב. D. ...הָאָרֶץ הַטּוֹבָה

‎E. ...מַלְכֵּנוּ הַטּוֹב. F. ...אֲבִיכֶם הַטּוֹב. G. ...הָאֲנָשִׁים הַטּוֹבִים.

‎4. A. שְׁמֵנוּ גָּדוֹל בָּאָרֶץ כִּי אֲנַחְנוּ אֲנָשִׁים טוֹבִים. B. שְׁמָהּ גָּדוֹל בָּאָרֶץ

‎כִּי הִיא אִשָּׁה טוֹבָה. C. שִׁמְךָ...אַתָּה אִישׁ טוֹב. D. שְׁמִי...אֲנִי אִישׁ טוֹב.

‎E. שִׁמְכֶם...אַתֶּם אֲנָשִׁים טוֹבִים. F. שְׁמָן...הֵנָּה נָשִׁים טוֹבוֹת.

‎5. A. רֻגַּח שָׁכְבָה בְּבֵיתָהּ וְזָכְרָה אֶת מְקוֹם מִשְׁפַּחְתָּהּ. B. בְּתֵּי שָׁכְבָה בְּבֵיתָהּ

‎וְזָכְרָה...מִשְׁפַּחְתָּהּ. C. בְּנָהּ שָׁכַב בְּבֵיתוֹ וְזָכַר...מִשְׁפַּחְתּוֹ. D. שָׁכַבְנוּ

‎בְּבֵיתֵנוּ וְזָכַרְנוּ...מִשְׁפַּחְתֵּנוּ. E. דּוֹדְכֶם שָׁכַב בְּבֵיתוֹ וְזָכַר...מִשְׁפַּחְתּוֹ.

‎F. הַנָּשִׁים שָׁכְבוּ בְּבֵיתָן וְזָכְרוּ...מִשְׁפַּחְתָּן.

1. Who is in my house with my son? A. Who is in your house with your son? B. ...in his house...his son? C. ...in our house...our son? D. ...in your house...your son? E. ...in her house...her son? F. ...in your house...your son? G. ...in your house...your son? H. ...in their house...their son? I. ...in their house...their son? 2. What is in my hand? My book is in my hand. A. What is in their hand? Their book is in their hand. B. ...your hand? Your book... C. ...our hand? Our book... D. ...their hand? Their book... E. ...your hand? Your book... F. ...his hand? His book... G. ...your hand? Your book... H. ...her hand? Her book... I. ...your hand? Your book... 3. I did not remember my good daughter. A. I did not remember her good son. B. ...his good mother. C. ...the good king. D. ...the good land. E. ...our good king. F. ...your good father. G. ...the good people. 4. His name is great in the land because he is a good man. A. Our name is great in the land because we are good people. B. Her name...she is a good woman. C. Your name...you are a good man. D. My name... I am a good man. E. Your name...you are good men. F. Their name...they are good women. 5. The man lay in his house and

remembered his family's place. A. Ruth lay in her house and remembered her family's place. B. My daughter lay in her house and remembered her family's place. C. Your son lay in his house and remembered his family's place. D. We lay in our house and remembered our family's place. E. Your uncle lay in his house and remembered his family's place. F. The women lay in their house and remembered their family's place.

Exercise 3 .1 אָכְלוֹ .2 דַּרְכְּכֶם .3 סִפְרִי .4 מִשְׁפַּחְתְּךָ .5 מַלְכָּהּ

.6 נַעֲרוֹ .7 בִּתְּכֶם .8 שְׁמָהּ .9 בְּנָהּ .10 אַרְצָן .11 לַחְמוֹ

Exercise 4 1. his wife 2. Who is her daughter? 3. my family 4. our king 5. Who is his father? 6. his shoe 7. What is in his hand? 8. their uncle 9. What is your name? 10. my mother's house 11. our good land 12. the voice of their judge

Exercise 5 "Goldilocks and the Three Bears" There were three bears that lived in their house in a big field. In the bears' family there was Father-Bear, Mother-Bear, and Son-Bear. In the morning, the bears went to their big field and there was not a bear in the bears' house. In the city there was a maiden and her name was Goldilocks. She went from her house in the city to the fields. She walked and walked and came to the bears' house. In the house was a table and on the table was food. There were also three chairs. Goldilocks sat on one chair and the chair was very big. She sat on the second chair and the second chair was also big. She sat on the third chair and the chair was good. Goldilocks sat on the chair and ate the food that was on the table. In the house were three beds. Goldilocks lay down on one bed and the bed was very big. She lay down on the second bed and it also was big. She lay down on the third bed and the bed was good. Goldilocks slept there. The bears came from their field to their house. They went to the table. Father-Bear said in his very big voice: "Who ate my food?" Mother-Bear said in her big voice: "Who ate my food?" Son-Bear said in a not-big voice: "Who ate my food?" The bears sat on the chairs. Father-Bear said in his very big voice:"Who sat on my chair?" Mother-Bear said in her big voice: "Who sat on my chair?" Son-Bear said in a not-big voice: "Who sat on my chair?" The bears walked to the beds. Father-Bear said in his very big voice: "Who lay down on my bed?" Mother-Bear said in her big voice: "Who lay down on my bed?" Son-Bear said in a not-big voice: "Who lay down on my bed? A maiden lay down on my bed and she is still in my bed!" The bears loved Goldilocks and she lived with the bears' family forever.

CHAPTER 14

Exercise 2 1. A. הַמֶּלֶךְ הַזָּקֵן שָׁמַר וְהוּא עוֹד שׁוֹמֵר. B. הַמֶּלֶךְ הַזָּקֵן

כָּתַב...כּוֹתֵב. C. ...שָׁמַע...שׁוֹמֵעַ. D. ...יָשַׁב...יוֹשֵׁב. E. ...שָׁכַב

שׁוֹכֵב. 2. A. בֹּעֲזִי פּוֹתֵחַ אֶת שַׁעֲרֵי עִירוֹ תַּחַת אַבְרָהָם. B. אֲנַחְנוּ

פּוֹתְחִים...עִירֵנוּ... C. אַתָּה פּוֹתֵחַ...עִירְךָ... D. הֵנָּה פּוֹתְחוֹת...

עִירָן... E. אֲנִי פּוֹתֵחַ...עִירִי... F. אַתֶּן פּוֹתְחוֹת...עִירְכֶן...

G. אַתְּ פּוֹתַחַת...עִירֵךְ... H. אַתֶּם פּוֹתְחִים...עִירְכֶם... 3. A. הַנְּעָרִים

הַקּוֹצְרִים לָקְחוּ אֶת הַמִּנְחָה מִן בֹּעַז. B. הַבֵּן הַקּוֹצֵר לָקַח... C. הַנָּשִׁים

הַקּוֹצְרוֹת לָקְחוּ... D. דָּוִד הַקּוֹצֵר לָקַח... E. אֲנַחְנוּ הַקּוֹצְרִים לָקַחְנוּ...

4. ... A. בְּנִי שׁוֹמֵעַ אֶת קוֹלִי כָּל הַלַּיְלָה. B. הֵם שׁוֹמְעִים...

C. הַנַּעֲרָה שׁוֹמַעַת... D. הַשּׁוֹמֵר שׁוֹמֵעַ... E. הַנָּשִׁים שׁוֹמְעוֹת...

5. A. שָׂרָה הָרָעָה לוֹקַחַת אֶת הָאֹכֶל מִתַּחַת בֵּיתֵנוּ. B. דּוֹדָתָהּ הָרָעָה

לוֹקַחַת... C. הַנְּעָרוֹת הָרָעוֹת לוֹקְחוֹת... D. הַשּׁוֹמְרִים הָרָעִים לוֹקְחִים

E. ... אֲנָשִׁים רָעִים לוֹקְחִים... 6. A. נַעֲלֵי הַמֶּלֶךְ שְׁמוּרִים כָּל הַיּוֹם

וְכָל הַלַּיְלָה. B. שְׂדֵי הַמֶּלֶךְ שָׁמוּר... C. בְּנוֹת הַמֶּלֶךְ שְׁמוּרוֹת...

D. כִּסֵּא הַמֶּלֶךְ שָׁמוּר... E. מְקוֹם הַמֶּלֶךְ שָׁמוּר...

1. The old king reigned and he is still reigning. A. The old
king guarded and he is still guarding. B. The old king wrote
...writing. C. ...heard...hearing. D. ...sat...sitting...
E. ...lay down....lying. 2. Boaz is opening the gates of
his city instead of Abraham. A. Naomi is opening the gates
of her city instead of Abraham. B. We are opening...our city
... C. You are opening...your city... D. They are opening...
their city... E. I am opening...my city... F. You are
opening...your city... G. You are opening...your city...
H. You are opening...your city... 3. The harvesting woman
took the gift from Boaz. A. The harvesting lads took the
gift from Boaz. B. The son who is harvesting took... C. The
harvesting women took... D. David who is harvesting took...
E. We who are harvesting took... 4. My son hears my
voice the whole night. A. Our daughter hears my voice
the whole night. B. They hear my voice... C. The
young woman hears... D. The guard hears... E. The
women hear... 5. The evil man is taking the

20

food from under our house. A. Evil Sarah is taking the food from under our house. B. Her evil aunt is taking... C. The evil maidens are taking... D. The evil guards are taking... E. The evil people are taking... 6. The king's house is guarded all day and all night. A. The king's shoes are guarded all day and all night. B. The king's field is guarded ... C. The king's daughters are guarded... D. The king's throne is guarded... E. The king's place is guarded...

Exercise 3 1. לָקוּחַ 2. שְׁלוּחוֹת 3. פְּתוּחִים 4. זָכוּר 5. שְׁמוּרָה

6. פָּתוּחַ 7. כָּתוּב 8. שְׁמוּרָה 9. זְכוּרִים

Exercise 4 1. דָּוִד שָׁמַר 2. פְּתַחְנוּ 3. הוּא מָלַךְ 4. הָלַכְתָּ

5. הַנָּשִׁים שָׁמַעְנוּ 6. הַמֶּלֶךְ הַזָּקֵן שָׁפַט 7. הֵנָּה לָקְחוּ 8. הָלַכְתִּי

1. David guarded the house instead of Jacob. 2. We opened the gate in the morning in front of the people of the city. 3. He ruled over all the land. 4. You went to the city instead of your mother. 5. We guarded the holy man in Bethlehem. 6. The old king judged the evil man in front of the nation. 7. They took the bread instead of the fruit. 8. I went after the harvesters.

Exercise 5 1. אֲנִי אוֹכֶלֶת עִם אִמִּי. 2. אַתָּה כּוֹתֵב מִבֵּיתוֹ. 3. הִיא

זוֹכֶרֶת אֶת הָאֲנָשִׁים בְּעִירָהּ. 4. הָאֹכֶל מֵעִירָהּ זָכוּר. 5. הָאֹכֶל הַטּוֹב

מִבֵּיתֵנוּ שָׁמוּר. 6. רוּת לָקְחָה אֶת דּוֹדָתָהּ לָעִיר הַגְּדוֹלָה. 7. בֹּעַז לָקַח

אֶת בְּנוֹ לְעִירוֹ.

Exercise 6 "The Farmer in the Dell"(harvester קוֹצֵר = farmer) The farmer in the field, the farmer in the field, heigh ho the derio, the farmer in the field. The farmer takes a wife, the farmer takes a wife, heigh ho the derio, the farmer takes a wife. The wife takes a son...heigh ho...the wife takes a son. The son takes a maiden...heigh ho...the son takes a maiden. The maiden takes bread...heigh ho...the maiden takes bread. The bread stands alone...heigh ho...the bread stands alone.

Exercise 7 1. כָּתַב 2. כּוֹתֵב 3. כָּתוּב 4. פָּתְחוּ 5. פּוֹתְחִים

6. פְּתוּחִים 7. קָצַרְתָּ 8. זְכַרְתֶּן 9. זוֹכְרוֹת

1. he wrote 2. writing 3. is written 4. they opened 5. opening 6. are opened 7. you harvested 8. you remembered 9. remembering

21

CHAPTER 15

Exercise 1 1. זֶה מָקוֹם גָּדוֹל וְטוֹב. B. זֹאת אֶרֶץ גְּדוֹלָה וְטוֹבָה A.
C. זֶה חֶסֶד גָּדוֹל וְטוֹב. D. אֵלֶּה שָׂדוֹת גְּדוֹלִים וְטוֹבִים. E. אֵלֶּה
עָרִים גְּדוֹלוֹת וְטוֹבוֹת. 2. A. אֵין לִי אֹכֶל כִּי יֵשׁ רָעָב בָּעִיר הַהִיא.
B. אֵין לָכֶן אֹכֶל... C. אֵין לוֹ אֹכֶל... D. אֵין לָהֶן... E. אֵין לָכֶם
... F. אֵין לָהּ... G. אֵין לְךָ... H. אֵין לָהֶם... I. אֵין לָךְ...
3. A. יַעֲקֹב שָׁמַע אֶת קוֹל הַמֶּלֶךְ הָרַע הַזֶּה. B. ...הַשּׁוֹפְטִים הָרָעִים הָאֵלֶּה
... C. ...הַדּוֹדָה הָרָעָה הַזֹּאת. D. ...הָאָבוֹת הָרָעִים הָאֵלֶּה... E. ...
...הַנָּשִׁים הָרָעוֹת הָאֵלֶּה. 4. A. יֵשׁ לִי סְפָרִים אֲשֶׁר אֲנִי לוֹקֵחַ מִמִּשְׁפַּחְתִּי.
B. ...יֵשׁ לַבָּנִים... הֵם לוֹקְחִים מִמִּשְׁפַּחְתָּם. C. ...יֵשׁ לָהּ...הִיא לוֹקַחַת
מִמִּשְׁפַּחְתָּהּ. D. ...יֵשׁ לָכֶם...אַתֶּם לוֹקְחִים מִמִּשְׁפַּחְתְּכֶם. E. ...יֵשׁ לָךְ... אַתְּ
לוֹקַחַת מִמִּשְׁפַּחְתֵּךְ. F. ...יֵשׁ לָהֶן...הֵנָּה לוֹקְחוֹת מִמִּשְׁפַּחְתָּן. G. ...יֵשׁ לְךָ...
אַתָּה לוֹקֵחַ מִמִּשְׁפַּחְתְּךָ. H. ...יֵשׁ לָכֶן...אַתֶּן לוֹקְחוֹת מִמִּשְׁפַּחְתְּכֶן. I. ...יֵשׁ
לָנוּ... אֲנַחְנוּ לוֹקְחִים מִמִּשְׁפַּחְתֵּנוּ. 5. A. זֹאת הַבַּת אֲשֶׁר פָּתְחָה אֶת
הַשְּׁעָרִים הַהֵמָּה. B. אֵלֶּה הָאֲנָשִׁים אֲשֶׁר פָּתְחוּ... C. ...זֹאת הַמִּשְׁפָּחָה אֲשֶׁר
פָּתְחָה... D. ...אֵלֶּה הָאִמּוֹת אֲשֶׁר פָּתְחוּ... E. זֶה הַדּוֹד אֲשֶׁר פָּתַח ...
6. A. אָמַרְתִּי דְּבָרִים טוֹבִים עַל אִמִּי. B. אֲמַרְתֶּם...אִמְּכֶם. C. הִיא
אָמְרָה...אִמָּהּ. D. הֵנָּה אָמְרוּ...אִמָּן. E. הוּא אָמַר...אִמּוֹ. F. אָמַרְנוּ
...אִמֵּנוּ. G. אֲמַרְתֶּן...אִמְּכֶן. H. אָמַרְתָּ...אִמְּךָ. I. הֵם אָמְרוּ...אִמָּם

1. This is a great and good nation. A. This is a great and
good place. B. This is a great and good land. C. This is a
great and good kindness. D. These are great and good fields.
E. These are great and good cities. 2. We don't have food
because there is a famine in that city. A. I don't have food
because there is a famine in that city. B. You don't have
food... C. He doesn't have food... D. They don't have food..
E. You don't have food... F. She doesn't have food... G. You
don't have food... H. They don't have food... I. You don't
have food... 3. Jacob heard this evil woman's voice.
A. Jacob heard this evil king's voice. B. ...these evil
judges' voice. C. ...this evil aunt's voice. D. ...these

22

evil fathers' voice. E. ...these evil women's voice.
4. He has books that he is taking from his family. A. I
have books that I am taking from my family. B. The sons
have...they are taking from their family. C. She has...
she is taking from her family. D. You have...you are taking
from your family. E. You have...you are taking from your
family. F. They have...they are taking from their family.
G. You have...you are taking from your family. H. You have..
you are taking from your family. I. We have...we are taking
from our family. 5. These are the judges that opened those
gates. A. This is the daughter that opened those gates.
B. These are the people that opened... C. This is the family
that opened... D. These are the mothers that opened...
E. This is the uncle that opened... 6. You said good things
about your mother. A. I said good things about my mother.
B. You said...your mother. C. She said...her mother. D. They
said...their mother. E. He said...his mother. F. We said...
our mother. G. You said...your mother. H. You said...your
mother. I. They said...their mother.

Exercise 2   1. יֵשׁ לִי סְפָרִים בַּבַּיִת. 2. יֵשׁ בַּיִת גָּדוֹל לָאֲנָשִׁים הָהֵמָּה.

3. יֵשׁ לַנַּעַר מִמּוֹאָב עֵינַיִם רָעוֹת וְיָדַיִם גְּדוֹלוֹת. 4. כָּל בֹּקֶר וְכָל לַיְלָה

יֵשׁ אֲנָשִׁים בַּדֶּרֶךְ. 5. הַיּוֹם אֵין לֶחֶם בָּעִיר. 6. בְּבֵית לֶחֶם יֵשׁ אִשָּׁה אֲשֶׁר

יוֹשֶׁבֶת בְּבַיִת גָּדוֹל.

1. I have books in the house. 2. Those people have a large
house. 3. The lad from Moab has evil eyes and big hands.
4. Every morning and every night there are people on the
road. 5. Today there is no bread in the city. 6. In Bethlehem
there is a woman who is staying in a big house.

Exercise 3   1. הָיוּ לָנוּ נַעֲלַיִם גְּדוֹלוֹת מְאֹד. 2. לֹא הָיוּ קוֹצְרִים

בַּשָּׂדֶה הַיּוֹם. 3. בַּמָּקוֹם הַהוּא לֹא הָיָה לְנָעֳמִי שָׂדֶה גָּדוֹל. 4. לִפְנֵי

אַבְרָהָם הָיָה שַׁעַר פָּתוּחַ. 5. הָיָה בָּאָרֶץ הַהִיא מֶלֶךְ טוֹב. 6. הָיָה לְךָ שֵׁם

טוֹב בַּמָּקוֹם הַזֶּה.

1. We had a very big pair of shoes. 2. There were no
harvesters in the field today. 3. Naomi did not have a big
field in that place. 4. In front of Abraham was an opened
gate. 5. There was a good king in that land. 6. You had a
good name in this place.

Exercise 4   1. הָאִישׁ הַזֶּה רַע. 2. הָאִישׁ הָרַע הַזֶּה מִמּוֹאָב. 3. הָאִישׁ

23

הָרַע הַהוּא מִמּוֹאָב אָבִיו. 4. אֵלֶּה נָשִׁים טוֹבוֹת. 5. הַנָּשִׁים הַטּוֹבוֹת

הֵהֵנָּה אִמּוֹת הַנְּעָרִים. 6. יֵשׁ וַאֲנָשִׁים גְּדוֹלִים בְּעִירִי. 7. אֵין אֲנָשִׁים

רָעִים בָּעִיר הַזֹּאת.

Exercise 5 1. הָלַךְ 2. אָכְלוּ 3. כָּתְבוּ 4. זָכַרְתָּ 5. שָׁכַבְתִּי, שָׁמַעְתִּי

6. אָמַר 7. מָלַךְ

1. Jacob's father went today after his wife. 2. Those
harvesters ate bread with those women. 3. Those maidens
wrote evil things instead of good things. 4. What did you
still remember about this place? 5. When I lay down at
night, I heard my mother's voice. 6. Who said a word of
kindness to that old woman? 7. One king ruled over the holy
cities and also over Moab.

1. הוֹלֵךְ 2. אֹכְלִים 3. כֹּתְבוֹת 4. זֹכֶרֶת 5. שׁוֹכֵב, שׁוֹמֵעַ 6. אוֹמֵר

7. מוֹלֵךְ

Exercise 6 This is the house that is in the field of Judah.
This is the man that lives in the house that is in the field
of Judah. This is the wife that lives with the man that lives
in... These are the daughters that belong to the wife...
These are the lads that take the daughters... This is the
judge that guards the lads... This is the famine that kills
the judge... This is the nation that weeps about the famine
that kills the judge that guards the lads that take the
daughters that belong to the wife that lives with the man
that lives in the house that is in the field of Judah.

Exercise 7 1. אָכַלְתִּי 2. אֹכֵל 3. זָכַרְנוּ 4. זֹכְרִים 5. הָלַכְתָּ

6. הוֹלֶכֶת 7. כְּתַבְתֶּן 8. כּוֹתְבוֹת 9. כְּתוּבוֹת 10. שָׁמַעְתְּ 11. שׁוֹמֵעַ

1. I ate 2. eating 3. we remembered 4. remembering 5. you
walked 6. walking 7. you wrote 8. writing 9. written 10. you
heard 11. hearing

CHAPTER 16

Exercise 2 1. A. תִּשְׁמֹרְנָה אֶת שַׁעֲרֵי הָעִיר. B. הֵם יִשְׁמְרוּ...

C. הִיא תִּשְׁמֹר D. אֶשְׁמֹר... E. תִּשְׁמְרוּ... F. הֵנָּה תִּשְׁמֹרְנָה...

G. תִּשְׁמֹר... H. נִשְׁמֹר... I. תִּשְׁמְרִי... 2. A. בַּעֲלֵי רוּחַ לֹא כְּנַעֲלֵי

אָמָּה. B. כִּסְאוֹת רוּת לֹא כְּכִסְאוֹת... C. סֵפֶר רוּת...כְּסֵפֶר... D. קוֹל

...כְּקוֹל. E. אֹכֶל...כְּאֹכֶל. 3. A. הֲעוֹד תִּזְכֹּרְנָה אֶת שֹׁפְטֵי הַמָּקוֹם

הַהוּא? B. הֲעוֹד הַנָּשִׁים תִּזְכֹּרְנָה... C. הֲעוֹד הַנַּעֲרָה תִּזְכֹּר... D. הֲעוֹד

תִּזְכְּרוּ... E. הֲעוֹד תִּזְכְּרִי... F. הֲעוֹד הָאַחִים יִזְכְּרוּ... G. הֲעוֹד

נִזְכֹּר... H. הֲעוֹד אֶזְכֹּר... 4. A. אִם לֹא יִכְתֹּב בַּסֵּפֶר, לֹא יִזְכֹּר אֶת

הַדְּבָרִים הָאֵלֶּה. B. אִם לֹא תִּכְתֹּבְנָה בַּסֵּפֶר, לֹא תִּזְכֹּרְנָה... C. אִם לֹא

נִכְתֹּב...לֹא נִזְכֹּר... D. ...תִּכְתְּבוּ...תִּזְכְּרוּ... E. ...אֶכְתֹּב...אֶזְכֹּר

... F. ...תִּכְתְּבִי...תִּזְכְּרִי... G. ...יִכְתְּבוּ...יִזְכְּרוּ...

5. A. אֵין לְאַבְרָהָם שָׂדוֹת בֵּין הֶהָרִים הָהֵם וּבֵין הָעִיר הַהִיא. B. ...

וּבֵין הַמָּקוֹם הַהוּא. C. ...וּבֵין הַשָּׂדֶה הַהוּא. D. ...וּבֵין הַדְּרָכִים

הָהֵמָּה. E. ...וּבֵין הַבַּיִת הַהוּא. 6. A. הִנֵּה בְּנוֹת אַבְרָהָם הַיּוֹשְׁבוֹת

בִּירוּשָׁלַם תִּשְׁלַחְנָה מִנְחָה אֶל מַלְכָּן. B. הִנֵּה הַמִּשְׁפָּחָה הַיּוֹשֶׁבֶת בִּירוּשָׁלַם

תִּשְׁלַח מִנְחָה אֶל מַלְכָּהּ. C. ...הָאָבוֹת הַיּוֹשְׁבִים...יִשְׁלְחוּ...מַלְכָּם.

D. ...הַשּׁוֹמֵר הַיּוֹשֵׁב...יִשְׁלַח...מַלְכּוֹ. E. ...בְּנֵי עַמִּי הַיּוֹשְׁבִים...

יִשְׁלְחוּ...מַלְכָּם.

1. He will guard the gates of the city. A. You will guard the
gates of the city. B. They will guard... C. She will guard...
D. I will guard... E. You will guard... F. They will guard...
G. You will guard... H. We will guard... I. You will guard...
2. Ruth's eyes are not like her mother's eyes. A. Ruth's
shoes are not like her mother's shoes. B. Ruth's chairs...her
mother's chairs. C. Ruth's book...her mother's book.
D. Ruth's voice...her mother's voice. E. Ruth's food...her
mother's food. 3. Will you still remember the judges of that
place? A. Will you still remember the judges of that place?
B. Will the women still remember... C. Will the maiden still
remember... D. Will you still remember... E. Will you still
remember... F. Will the brothers still remember... G. Will we
still remember... H. Will I still remember... 4. If you do
not write in the book, you will not remember these words.
A. If he does not write in the book, he will not remember
these words. B. If you do not write in the book, you will not
remember... C. If we do not write...we will not remember...
D. If you do not write...you will not remember... E. If I do
not write...I will not remember... F. If you do not write...

25

you will not remember... G. If they do not write...they will
not remember... 5. Abraham does not have fields between those
mountains and that city. A. Abraham does not have fields
between those mountains and that place. B. ...and that field.
C. ...and those roads. D. ...and that house. 6. Behold, that
man who is staying in Jerusalem will send a gift to his king.
A. Behold, the daughters of Abraham who are staying in
Jerusalem will send a gift to their king. B. Behold, the
family who is staying in Jerusalem will send a gift to its
king. C. Behold, the fathers who are staying...will send...
their king. D. Behold, the guard who is staying...will send..
his king. E. Behold, Naomi's sons who are staying...will send
...their king.

Exercise 3 1. תִּקְצֹר, קָצַרְתָּ, קוֹצֵר 2. תִּשְׁכַּב, שָׁכְבָה, שׁוֹכֶבֶת

3. יִשְׁלְחוּ, שָׁלְחוּ, שׁוֹלְחִים 4. תִּשְׁמַעְנָה, שָׁמְעוּ, שׁוֹמְעוֹת 5. יִכְתֹּב,

פָּתַב, כּוֹתֵב 6. תִּזְכֹּרְנָה, זְכַרְתֶּן, זוֹכְרוֹת

1. You will harvest in the morning in the field. 2. At night,
Abraham's wife will lie down on her bed in Ruth's house.
3. After the famine, Sarah's brothers will send food to their
father in Judah. 4. The women from Moab will hear these words
from the king. 5. Behold, the head of the house will write to
those maidens. 6. You will remember the name of the woman
who is sitting in front of those men.

Exercise 4 1. תִּשְׁמַע 2. הַתְקֹצֹר 3. נִזְכֹּר 4. תִּשְׁלַחְנָה 5. יִמְלֹךְ,

נִשְׁמַע

Exercise 5 1. הַנַּעֲרָה תִּזְכֹּר אֶת הָאִישׁ הָרַע. 2. אֲחִי הַנַּעֲרָה יִשְׁמַע אֶת

קוֹל הָאִישׁ הָרַע. 3. אֲבִי הַנַּעֲרָה וְדוֹדָהּ יִשְׁמְרוּ אֶת הָאֲנָשִׁים הָרָעִים.

4. דָּוִד אִישׁ רַע בָּאָרֶץ הַהִיא. 5. אֵין אֲנָשִׁים רָעִים בְּבֵיתֵנוּ.

6. הֲתִזְכְּרִי אֶת אַנְשֵׁי עִירֵנוּ הַטּוֹבִים?

Exercise 6 1. If I send Ruth to the top of the mountain,
will you send Sarah? 2. If you judge between the brothers,
will you also judge between this lad and his father? 3. If we
harvest in the field, we will not hear the words of the women
in the tent. 4. Will they obey the king, if he is an evil
king? 5. If you lie on your bed all day, you will not write
your book.

Exercise 7 The lad said: When I am a man, I will rule over
all my land. I will rule from the mountains as far as the sea

in peace. I will send good judges to all the cities, and they will judge the evil people. On that day, they will send those people from the land. I will remember my family: my father and my mother and my brother and my uncle and my aunt. I will send them bread. All the women will obey me. My people will send me gifts. Great men will guard my house. I will lie in a bed better than all the beds in my land. When I am a man, I will be the king, because today I am the son of the king.

Exercise 8   1. שָׁכַב   2. יִשְׁכַּב   3. שׁוֹכֵב   4. פָּתְחָה   5. תִּשְׁמֹר

6. שׁוֹמֶרֶת   7. שָׁמַעְתָּ   8. תִּשְׁמְעִי   9. שׁוֹמֵעַ   10. נִזְכֹּר   11. תִּזְכְּרוּ

12. יִזְכֹּר   13. תִּזְכֹּרְנָה   14. זוֹכְרִים   15. זָכְרוּ   16. תִּשְׁפֹּט

17. תִּשְׁפֹּט   18. שָׁפְטָה   19. תִּשְׁפְּטִי   20. כָּתַבְנוּ   21. נִכְתֹּב

22. כְּתוּבִים   23. תִּכְתְּבִי   24. תִּכְתֹּבְנָה

1. he lay down 2. he will lie down 3. lying 4. she opened 5. she will guard 6. guarding 7. you heard 8. you will hear 9. hearing 10. we will remember 11. you will remember 12. he will remember 13. they will remember 14. remembering 15. they remembered 16. you will judge 17. she will judge 18. she judged 19. you will judge 20. we wrote 21. we will write 22. written 23. you will write 24. they will write

CHAPTER 17

Exercise 2   1. A. קְחִי אֶת דָּוִד לְמֶלֶךְ פַּתַח הָאִישׁ הָרַע הַזֶּה. B. קַחֲנָה

אֶת דָּוִד ...   C. קְחוּ אֶת דָּוִד ...   2. A. אַל תִּבְטַח בְּדִבְרֵי הַשּׁוֹפְטִים.

B. אַל תִּבְטְחִי ...   C. אַל תִּבְטְחֶנָה ...   3. A. נִלְבְּשָׁה בְּגָדִים וְנַעֲלַיִם

מִבֵּית מִשְׁפַּחְתֵּנוּ.   B. נִבְחֲרָה ...   C. נִשְׁלְחָה ...   D. נִזְכְּרָה ...

4. A. לְכִי וּשְׁבִי בְּבֵיתֵךְ וְשִׁמְעִי בְּקוֹל אִמֵּךְ.   B. לְכוּ וּשְׁבוּ בְּבֵיתְכֶם

וְשִׁמְעוּ בְּקוֹל אִמְּכֶם.   C. לֵכְבָה וְשֵׁבְנָה בְּבֵיתְכֶן וּשְׁמַעְנָה בְּקוֹל אִמְּכֶן.

5. A. הַנַּעֲרָה תִּקַּח אֶת מִנְחָתָהּ אֶל הָאִישׁ הֶחָכָם הַיּוֹשֵׁב בַּשָּׂדֶה.   B. רָאשֵׁי הָעָם

יִקְחוּ אֶת מִנְחָתָם ...   C. תִּקַּח אֶת מִנְחָתְךָ ...   D. אֶקַּח אֶת מִנְחָתִי ...   E. נְשֵׁי

יְרוּשָׁלַיִם תִּקַּחְנָה אֶת מִנְחָתָן ...   F. נִקַּח אֶת מִנְחָתֵנוּ ...   G. תִּקַּחְנָה אֶת

27

מִנְחָתְכֶן... H. תְּקְחוּ אֶת מִנְחַתְכֶם... I. תִּקְחִי אֶת מִנְחָתֵךְ...

1. Take David to a king instead of this evil man. A. Take David to a king instead of this evil man. B. Take David...C. Take David... 2. Do not trust the words of the judges. A. Do not trust the words of the judges. B. Do not trust... C. Do not trust... 3. Let us steal clothes and shoes from our family's house. A. Let us put on clothes and shoes from our family's house. B. Let us choose clothes... C. Let us send... D. Let us remember... 4. Go and sit in your house and obey your mother. A. Go and sit in your house and obey your mother. B. Go and sit in your house and obey your mother. C. Go and sit in your house and obey your mother. 5. Abraham will take his gift to the wise man sitting in the field. A. The maiden will take her gift to the wise man sitting in the field. B. The heads of the people will take their gift... C. You will take your gift... D. I will take my gift... E. The women of Jerusalem will take their gift... F. We will take our gift... G. You will take your gift... H. You will take your gift... I. You will take your gift...

Exercise 3 1. לְבַשׁ, אַל תִּלְבַּשׁ 2. לְכִנָה, אַל תֵּלַכְנָה 3. גִּנְבוּ, אַל
תִּגְנְבוּ 4. קְחִי, אַל תִּקְחִי 5. שְׁכַחְנָה, אַל תִּשְׁכַּחְנָה 6. בְּטַח, אַל תִּבְטַח
7. שִׁמְעוּ, אַל תִּשְׁמְעוּ 8. שְׁפֹט, אַל תִּשְׁפֹּט 9. בְּחַר, אַל תִּבְחַר

1. Put on your clothes! 2. Go from your city to that city! 3. Steal the clothes, because the old one is guarding the house! 4. Take the fruit of the land! 5. Forget the things that I said! 6. Trust in your brother's kindness! 7. Obey him! 8. Judge all the people of the land! 9. Choose that maiden for a wife!

Exercise 4 1. לְכוּ 2. שְׁלַח 3. יִשְׁכַּב 4. תִּקַּחְנָה 5. נִקְצְרָה
6. אֶכְתְּבָה 7. לְכִי 8. דְּעוּ

1. Go to the top of the mountain! 2. Send fruit from the people of the city to the head of the city! 3. May the lad lie down at night in his family's house! 4. Let the wise women take fruit for themselves! 5. Let us harvest in the morning in the big fields! 6. Let me write a book like the book of my beloved! 7. Go on the road between the mountains until the sea! 8. Know the names of the fruit of the land of Israel.

Exercise 5 After King David, Solomon his son reigned over the land of Israel. He was very wise, and he was also a good judge. In those days, the people of Israel went to

Jerusalem to see Solomon the king. Among all the people that
went to Jerusalem there were two women. The name of the
first was Sarah and the name of the second was Orpah. There
was one lad between Sarah and Orpah when they came before
the king. Sarah said to Solomon: "This lad is not my son, he
is the son of this woman." Sarah said to Orpah: "Take your
son!" Orpah said: "He is not my son, I have no sons! Don't
you know that he is your son? Don't forget your son!" Sarah
said: "I remember my family and this lad is not from my
family." The two women said to Solomon: "Judge between us;
choose the mother of the lad!" King Solomon said to the
women: "Trust in the words of your king. Sit down, and obey
me. There is no mother in my land that does not remember her
son. If you do not remember this lad, he is not your son. Go
on your way. The lad will stay in my house." The king said
to the lad: "Forget these evil women! Stay in my house with
my family and wear the clothes of a king's son." The two
women said together: "He's my son! He's my son!" The king
said to the women: "I have judged! The lad will stay in my
house, go to your home!"

תִּפְתְּחִי .5 שְׁלַחְנָה .4 תִּשְׁלַחְנָה .3 שְׁפֹט .2 תִּשְׁפֹּט .1 Exercise 6

יֵלֵךְ .11 לְכוּ .10 יֵלְכוּ .9 גְּנֹבוּ .8 תִּגְנְבוּ .7 פְּתְחִי .6

דַּע .18 קַח .17 שְׁבִי .16 לְכִי .15 יֵדַע .14 יְקַח .13 יֵשֵׁב .12

שְׁמַעְנָה .19

1. you will judge 2. judge! 3. you will send 4. send! 5. you
will open 6. open! 7. you will steal 8. steal! 9. they will
go 10. go! 11. he will go 12. he will sit 13. he will take
14. he will know 15. go! 16. sit! 17. take! 18. know!
19. hear!

CHAPTER 18

בְּטַח, .4 שָׁפֹט שְׁפֹט, כָּתֹב פָּתֹח, .2 זָכֹר זְכֹר, .1 Exercise 1
מָלֹךְ מְלֹךְ, .8 לָכֵת לְכֵת, .7 שָׁלֹחַ שְׁלֹחַ, .6 לָקֹחַ קַחַת, .5 בָּטֹחַ

יָדֹעַ דַּעַת, .9

יְכַלְתֶּם .2 הָהָר. רֹאשׁ עַד מֵהַיָּם לָלֶכֶת יָכְלוּ הַבָּנִים .1 Exercise 2
בְּנָהּ. פְּנֵי אֶת לִזְכֹּר נוּכַל .3 הַהוּא. בַּמָּקוֹם הַקּוֹצְרִים בֵּין לִהְיוֹת
הָאֲנָשִׁים בֵּין לָשֶׁבֶת הֲתוּכַל .5 הַשָּׁמַיִם. תַּחַת בַּשָּׂדֶה בַּלַּיְלָה לִשְׁכַּב יְכָלְתָּ .4

29

הָאֵלֶּה?

1. The sons were able to walk from the sea until the top of
the mountain. 2. You were able to be among the harvesters in
that place. 3. We will be able to remember your son's face.
4. You were able to lie down at night in the field under the
heavens. 5. Will you be able to stay among these people?

Exercise 3 .1 A. הָאַחִים יָכְלוּ לִשְׁמֹר בְּתוֹךְ הַשָּׂדֶה. B. הָאַחִים יָכְלוּ

לִשְׁכַּב... C. ...לָשֶׁבֶת... D. ...לָלֶכֶת... E. ...לִהְיוֹת...

2. A. שָׁכוֹחַ תִּשְׁכַּח אֶת בֵּית אָבִיךָ. B. יָדוֹעַ תֵּדַע... C. בָּחוֹר תִּבְחַר...

D. שָׁמוֹר תִּשְׁמֹר... 3. A. שָׁמוֹר שָׁמַרְתָּ אֶת הַדְּבָרִים הָאֵלֶּה. B. שָׁמוֹר

שְׁמַרְנוּ... C. הֵמָּה שָׁמוֹר שָׁמְרוּ... D. הִיא שָׁמוֹר שָׁמְרָה... E. הֵם

שָׁמוֹר שָׁמְרוּ... 4. A. כְּלַבֹּשׁ אַבְרָהָם אֶת בִּגְדוֹ, יָשַׁב עַל כִּסְאוֹ. B. כִּלְבֹּשׁ

שָׂרָה אֶת בִּגְדָהּ, יָשְׁבָה עַל כִּסְאָהּ. C. כִּלְבֹּשׁ הַזְּקֵנָה אֶת בִּגְדָהּ, יָשְׁבָה עַל

כִּסְאָהּ. D. כִּלְבֹּשׁ בִּתִּי אֶת בִּגְדָהּ, יָשְׁבָה עַל כִּסְאָהּ. E. כִּלְבֹּשׁ הָאֵם אֶת

בִּגְדָהּ, יָשְׁבָה עַל כִּסְאָהּ. 5. A. בְּפָתְחָם אֶת הַשַּׁעַר, הֵמָּה שָׁמְעוּ אֶת קוֹל אַנְשֵׁי

עִירָם. B. בְּפָתְחֲךָ אֶת הַשַּׁעַר, שָׁמַעְתָּ אֶת קוֹל אַנְשֵׁי עִירְךָ. C. בְּפָתְחָהּ...

שָׁמְעָה נָעֳמִי...עִירָהּ. D. בְּפָתְחֵנוּ...שָׁמַעְנוּ...עִירֵנוּ. E. בְּפָתְחָן...

שָׁמְעוּ הַנְּעָרוֹת...עִירָן. F. בְּפָתְחֲכֶם...שְׁמַעְתֶּם...עִירְכֶם. G. בְּפָתְחֵךְ...

שָׁמַעְתְּ...עִירֵךְ. H. בְּפָתְחֲכֶן...שְׁמַעְתֶּן...עִירְכֶן. I. בְּפָתְחִי...שָׁמַעְתִּי...

עִירִי. 6 A. אוּכַל לִשְׁכַּב תַּחַת הָעֵץ הַקָּטֹן. B. הֵמָּה יוּכְלוּ לִשְׁכַּב...

C. תּוּכַלְנָה... D. רוּחַ תּוּכַל... E. אַתָּה וְדָוִד תּוּכְלוּ... F. נוּכַל...

G. תּוּכַל... H. תּוּכְלִי... I. הֵנָּה תּוּכַלְנָה...

1. The brothers were able to harvest in the midst of the
field. A. The brothers were able to guard in the midst of the
field. B. ...to lie down... C. ...to sit... D. ...to walk...
E. ...to be... 2. You will surely remember the house of your
father. A. You will surely forget the house of your father.
B. You will surely know... C. You will surely choose...
D. You will surely guard... 3. He surely kept these words.
A. You surely kept these words. B. We surely kept... C. They
surely kept... D. She surely kept... E. They surely kept...
4. As the maiden put on her garment, she sat on her chair.

A. As Abraham put on his garment, he sat on his chair. B. As
Sarah put on her garment, she sat on her chair. C. As the old
one put on her garment, she sat on her chair. D. As my
daughter put on her garment, she sat on her chair. E. As the
mother put on her garment, she sat on her chair. 5. When he
opened the gate, the guard heard the sound of the men of his
city. A. When they opened the gate, they heard the sound of
the men of their city. B. When you opened...you heard...your
city. C. When she opened...Naomi heard...her city. D. When
we opened...we heard...our city. E. When they opened...the
maidens...their city. F. When you opened...you heard...your
city. G. When you opened...you heard...your city. H. When you
opened...you heard...your city. I. When I opened...I heard...
my city. 6. The lad will be able to lie down under the small
tree. A. I will be able to lie down under the small
tree. B. They will be able... C. You will be able... D. Ruth will
be able... E. You and David will be able... F. We will be
able... G. You will be able... H. You will be able... I. They
will be able...

לִשְׁמֹר 5. מָלוֹךְ 4. לִקְצֹר 3. לִבְטֹחַ 2. לִשְׁכַּח 1. Exercise 4

פָּתֹחַ 8. לָשֶׁבֶת 7. גְּנֹב 6.

1. He was not able to forget the face of the maiden. 2. We
did not know if we were able to trust this judge. 3. He went
in the morning to harvest in the field. 4. You will surely
reign over all that is under the heavens. 5. The women were
not able to guard their house, and the lads stole everything.
6. While the men stole the food, they did not take the fruit.
7. When the sun is in the midst of the sky, our daughter will
be able to sit under the tree. 8. You will surely open the
gate of the city today - don't forget!

לֹא נוּכַל 2. הָאַחִים יוּכְלוּ לָלֶכֶת עַד הֶהָרִים הַהֵמָּה. 1. Exercise 5

לָלֶכֶת עַד הַיָּם. 3. הִיא תּוּכַל לָלֶכֶת עַד בֵּית דּוֹדָתָהּ. 4. הַחֲכָמִים יוּכְלוּ

לִשְׁפֹּט בֵּין הַמִּשְׁפָּחוֹת הָאֵלֶּה. 5. לֹא יָכֹלְתִּי לִשְׁפֹּט בֵּין בָּנֵי וּבֵין אָחִי.

6. יָכֹלְתָּ לִשְׁפֹּט בֵּין דּוֹדָתְךָ וּבֵין בִּתָּהּ. 7. לֹא תּוּכְלוּ לִבְחֹר כְּסֵא בַּמָּקוֹם

הַזֶּה. 8. לֹא הָיָה לְדָוִד כְּסֵא וְלֹא יָכֹל לָשֶׁבֶת. 9. לֹא הָיוּ לַמִּשְׁפָּחוֹת

פָּתִים וְהִנֵּה לֹא יָכְלוּ לָשֶׁבֶת בָּאָרֶץ. 10. הַנְּעָרוֹת הַקְּטַנּוֹת לֹא יָכְלוּ לִשְׁמֹעַ

אֶת דִּבְרֵי דּוֹדָן. 11. תּוּכְלִי לִשְׁמֹעַ אֶת קוֹל שָׂרָה. 12. לֹא יְכָלְתֶּן לִשְׁמֹעַ

אֶת דִּבְרֵי בִּתְּכֶן.

31

Exercise 6   "The Little Camel That Could"   In the city that was on the top of the mountain, there was a famine and the people there had no bread. They sent a man from the city on the mountain to a city that was by the sea. When they sent the man, they said to him: " Take your camel and go to that city because we have heard that there is food there. Don't forget that we have trusted you to bring us bread." The man went with his camel to the city by the sea and took food from there. When he took the food, he still remembered the famine in his city, and he did not lie down to rest. He went with his camel on the road to the mountains. And the sun in the sky was very hot. After he walked all morning, the camel lay down on the road and couldn't walk any more. The man said to his camel: Do not lie down on the road! Obey me! The people of the mountain are trusting in you!" The camel said to him: "I cannot go." The camel still lay down. The man said to himself: "If I do not take food to the people on the mountain they will die." And behold, a very big camel came on the road. The man said to the big camel: "There is a famine in the city in the mountains and the people of the city will die if I am not able to bring this food to them. My camel has completely lain down in the road and he is not able to walk. Will you be able to take the food and go to the top of the mountain?" The very big camel opened his mouth and said: "What are you saying to me? I am a very great camel! I go every day and every night to very great cities. I will not go to small towns that are in the mountains!" And he went on his way. And behold, the king's camel came on the road. The man said to the king's camel: "Listen, camel! There is a famine in the city in the mountains and the people of the city will die if I am not able to bring this food to them. My camel has completely lain down in the road and he is not able to walk. Will you be able to take the food and go to the top of the mountain?" The king's camel opened his mouth and said: "What are you saying to me? I am the king's camel! I go every day and every night to take only the king." And he went on his way. And behold, a very small camel came on the road. The man said to himself: "My camel is big and he was not able to go on this road. This camel is very small. He will not be able to go as far as the top of the mountain." But the man opened his mouth and said to the small camel: " Listen, little camel! There is a famine in the city in the mountains. The people of the city will die if you will not go as far as the top of the mountain to bring them food. Will you be able to go as far as the top of the mountain with the food?" The small camel said: "I surely can!" The small camel took the food from the camel that was lying down, and he and the man went on the road to the mountains. The sun in the sky was very hot and they walked and walked. The little camel said to himself: "I surely can! I surely can!" And the sun in the sky was very hot and they still walked. The little camel said to

himself: "I surely can!" But he was very weary. At night they
came to the city in the mountains. All the people of the city
ate from the food that was upon the little camel. The little
camel said to himself: "The big camel couldn't, the very big
camel couldn't, even the king's camel couldn't, but I really
could!"

CHAPTER 19

Exercise 1 1. his lad 2. your wife 3. their gifts 4. our
books 5. your house 6. your dwelling place 7. her stones
8. our land 9. my beasts 10. their fathers 11. your nation
12. her bread 13. your sons 14. his eyes 15. your hands
16. my tents 17. their gate 18. our light 19. your mother
20. my father

Exercise 2a 1. אַתְּ 2. הֵם 3. הִיא 4. אַתֶּן 5. אֲנִי 6. הֵנָּה

7. הוּא 8. אַתֶּם 9. אַתָּה

Exercise 2b 1. אֹתָךְ 2. אֶתְכֶם 3. אֹתוֹ 4. אֹתָן 5. אֹתִי 6. אֶתְכֶן

7. אֹתָהּ 8. אֹתָם 9. אֹתָךְ 10. אֹתָנוּ

Exercise 3 1. A. הוּא רַק שָׁכַח אֶת נְעָלָיו. B. רַק שְׁכַחְתֶּם אֶת
נַעֲלֵיכֶם. C. רַק שָׁכַחְתִּי אֶת נְעָלַי. D. רַק שְׁכַחְנוּ אֶת נַעֲלֵינוּ. E. הִיא
רַק שָׁכְחָה אֶת נְעָלֶיהָ. F. הֵם רַק שָׁכְחוּ אֶת נַעֲלֵיהֶם. G. רַק שְׁכַחְתֶּן אֶת
נַעֲלֵיכֶן. H. הֵנָּה רַק שָׁכְחוּ אֶת נַעֲלֵיהֶן. I. רַק שָׁכַחְתָּ אֶת נְעָלֶיךָ.
2. A. תֵּלְכִי לַמִּדְבָּר לָשֶׁבֶת שָׁם עִם בָּנַיִךְ. B. יֵלְכוּ...בְּנֵיהֶם. C. אֵלֵךְ...
בָּנַי. D. יֵלֵךְ...בָּנָיו. E. הָלַכְנוּ...בָּנֵינוּ. F. תֵּלַכְנָה...בְּנֵיכֶן.
G. הָלַכְתִּי...בָּנַי. 3. A. אַבְרָהָם לָקַח רַק אֶת בְּגָדָיו לְשַׁלַּח אֹתָם אֶל
מִשְׁפַּחְתּוֹ. B. הֵנָּה לָקְחוּ רַק אֶת בִּגְדֵיהֶן...מִשְׁפְּחוֹתֵיהֶן. C. לָקַחְתִּי רַק אֶת
בְּגָדַי...מִשְׁפַּחְתִּי. D. לְקָחֶתם רַק אֶת בִּגְדֵיכֶם...מִשְׁפְּחוֹתֵיכֶם. E. רוּת לָקְחָה
רַק אֶת בְּגָדֶיהָ...מִשְׁפַּחְתָּהּ. F. הַזְּקֵנִים לָקְחוּ רַק אֶת בִּגְדֵיהֶם...מִשְׁפְּחוֹתֵיהֶם
G. לָקַחְנוּ רַק אֶת בְּגָדֵינוּ...מִשְׁפְּחוֹתֵינוּ. H. לָקַחְתָּ רַק אֶת בְּגָדֶיךָ...
מִשְׁפַּחְתְּךָ. I. לְקַחְתֶּן רַק אֶת בִּגְדֵיכֶן...מִשְׁפְּחוֹתֵיכֶן. 4. A. בָּנֵי זָכְרוּ

33

אֹתְךָ וְאַתָּה לֹא זָכַרְתָּ אֹתָם. B. זְכַרְנוּ אֹתְךָ וְאַתָּה לֹא זָכַר אֹתָנוּ. C. אִמְּךָ

זָכְרָה...אֹתָהּ. D. הוּא זָכַר...אֹתוֹ. E. נְשֵׁי הָעִיר זָכְרוּ...אֹתָן.

5. A. כָּל דְּבָרֶיךָ הָיוּ בְּבָתֵּי עֵץ וְאַתָּה לָקַחְתָּ אֹתָם לְבָתֵּי אֲבָנִים. B. כָּל

דְּבָרֵיהֶם...וְהֵמָּה לָקְחוּ... C. כָּל דְּבָרָיו...וְהוּא לָקַח... D. כָּל

דְּבָרֵיכֶם...וּלְקַחְתֶּם... E. כָּל דְּבָרֶיהָ...וְלָקְחָה... 6. A. הֵם יִהְיוּ

בְּמִשְׁכַּנְכֶם הַיּוֹם וְיִשְׁמְרוּ אֶת בְּנֵיהֶם. B. תִּהְיִי בְּמִשְׁכָּנֵךְ הַיּוֹם וְתִשְׁמְרִי אֶת

בָּנַיִךְ. C. הָיִינוּ בְּמִשְׁכָּנֵנוּ הַיּוֹם וְשָׁמַרְנוּ אֶת בָּנֵינוּ. D. תִּהְיֶינָה

בְּמִשְׁכַּנְכֶן הַיּוֹם וְתִשְׁמֹרְנָה אֶת בְּנֵיכֶן. E. הִיא הָיְתָה בְּמִשְׁכָּנָהּ הַיּוֹם

וְשָׁמְרָה אֶת בָּנֶיהָ. F. תִּהְיוּ בְּמִשְׁכַּנְכֶם הַיּוֹם וְתִשְׁמְרוּ אֶת בְּנֵיכֶם.

G. הֵנָּה תִּהְיֶינָה בְּמִשְׁכָּנָן הַיּוֹם וְתִשְׁמֹרְנָה אֶת בְּנֵיהֶן. H. תִּהְיֶה בְּמִשְׁכָּנָהּ

הַיּוֹם וְתִשְׁמֹר אֶת בָּנֶיהָ. I. הוּא יִהְיֶה בְּמִשְׁכָּנוֹ הַיּוֹם וְיִשְׁמֹר אֶת בָּנָיו.

1. You only forgot your shoes. A. He only forgot his shoes.
B. You only forgot your shoes. C. I only forgot my shoes.
D. We only forgot our shoes. E. She only forgot her shoes.
F. They only forgot their shoes. G. You only forgot your
shoes. H. They only forgot their shoes. I. You only forgot
your shoes. 2. You will go to the wilderness to settle there
with your sons. A. You will go to the wilderness to settle
there with your sons. B. They will go to the wilderness to
settle there with their sons. C. I will go...my sons. D. He
will go...his sons. E. We went...our sons. F. You will go...
your sons. G. I went...my sons. 3. The judges took only
their clothes to send them to their families. A. Abraham
took only his clothes to send them to his family. B. They
took only their clothes to send them to their families.
C. I took only my clothes...my family. D. You took only your
clothes...your families. E. Ruth took only her clothes...her
family. F. The old ones took only their clothes...their
families. G. We took only our clothes...our families. H. You
took only your clothes...your family. I. You took only your
clothes...your families. 4. I remembered you and you did not
remember me. A. My sons remembered you and you did not
remember them. B. We remembered you and you did not remember
us. C. Your mother remembered you and you did not remember
her. D. He remembered....not remember him. E. The women of
the city...not remember them. 5. All their things were in
houses of wood and they took them to houses of stone. A. All
your things were in houses of wood and you took them to
houses of stone. B. All their things...and they took them...

34

C. All his things...and he took them... D. All your things..
and you took them... E. All your things...and you took them.
.. 6. I will be in my dwelling place today and I will guard
my sons. A. They will be in their dwelling place today and
they will guard their sons. B. You will be in your dwelling
place today and you will guard your sons. C. We were in our
dwelling place today and we guarded our sons. D. You will be
in your dwelling place today and you will guard your sons.
E. She was in her dwelling place today and she guarded her
sons. F. You will be in your dwelling place today and you
will guard your sons. G. They will be in their dwelling
place today and they will guard their sons. H. You will be
in your dwelling place today and you will guard your sons.
I. He will be in his dwelling place today and he will guard
his sons.

Exercise 4   1. אֹתוֹ   2. אֹתָם   3. אֹתָם   4. אֹתָהּ   5. אֹתָנוּ   6. אֶתְכֶן

7. אֹתוֹ   8. אֹתוֹ

1. They are eating it. 2. Don't forget that I remember them.
3. You will wear them. 4. In the darkness he lay in the
wilderness and remembered her. 5. He regularly will guard
us. 6. In the midst of that city, there will be wise ones
and they will judge you. 7. He wrote it by the light of
the sun. 8. The nations chose it and they settled there.

Exercise 5   1a. הוּא שָׁלַח אֶת הָאֲנָשִׁים אֶל בֵּיתוֹ.   1b. הוּא שָׁלַח אֹתָם

אֶל בֵּיתָם.   1c. הוּא שָׁלַח אֹתָם אֶל בָּתֵּיהֶם.   2a. הַנְּעָרִים לָקְחוּ אֶת

מִנְחָתָם וְשָׁלְחוּ אֹתָהּ אֶל אִמָּם.   2b. הַנְּעָרִים לָקְחוּ אֶת מִנְחוֹתֵיהֶם וְשָׁלְחוּ

אֹתָן אֶל אִמָּם.   2c. הַנְּעָרִים לָקְחוּ אֶת מִנְחוֹתֵיהֶם וְשָׁלְחוּ אֹתָן אֶל

אִמּוֹתֵיהֶם.   3a. הָאִשָּׁה תֵּשֵׁב בִּמְקוֹמָהּ וְתִשְׁמַע אֶת דְּבַר בְּנָהּ.   3b. הָאִשָּׁה

תֵּשֵׁב בִּמְקוֹמָהּ וְתִשְׁמַע אֶת דִּבְרֵי בָּנֶיהָ.   3c. הָאִשָּׁה תֵּשֵׁב בִּמְקוֹמָהּ וְתִשְׁמַע

אֹתָם.   4a. בַּיּוֹם יֵשׁ אוֹר וּבַלַּיְלָה יִהְיֶה חֹשֶׁךְ.   4b. הַגּוֹי הַזֶּה יֵלֵךְ רַק

בָּאוֹר וְלֹא יֵלֵךְ בַּחֹשֶׁךְ.   4c. הַגּוֹי הַזֶּה הָלַךְ מֵהַמִּדְבָּר עַד הַיָּם.

Exercise 6   "Little Red Riding Hood"   There was a small
maiden and her name was Little Red Riding Hood because she
regularly wore a red riding hood. She lived in the midst of
the city with her mother and her brother in a small stone
house. Her mother said to her: "Go to the tent of your
grandmother who is in the wilderness to take to her bread
and fruit. Walk only on the road, and not in the fields, and
don't trust strangers." Little Red Riding Hood said: "I will

obey you" and she went on her way. And behold, an evil beast
was in the midst of the wilderness. As Little Red Riding
Hood walked on the road in the wilderness, the evil beast
saw her and it said to itself: "Who is this small maiden?
And what are the things that are in her hands?" The beast
went to the maiden and said to her: "What are the things
that are in your hands? And where are you going?" Little Red
Riding Hood forgot everything that her mother had said to
her. She said: "I am going to my grandmother's tent to bring
her bread and fruit." The evil beast said to itself: "I will
go there to take everything: the old one, the food, and
Little Red Riding Hood." The beast went on another road to
the grandmother's tent. Little Red Riding Hood went on her
way and she came to her grandmother's tent. She said: "My
grandmother! Behold, good food!" She heard a voice from
inside the tent. "Little Red Riding Hood! Come in and I will
take it from your hands." Little Red Riding Hood did not
remember this voice and she said: "Are you my grandmother?"
And behold, she heard a voice from the tent: "Come into the
tent, and you will know that I am your grandmother." Little
Red Riding Hood went into the middle of the tent. When she
was in the tent, she saw the beast in her grandmother's bed.
Little Red Riding Hood did not know that the beast had eaten
her grandmother and put on her clothes. Little Red Riding
Hood said: "How big your eyes are!" The beast said: "With my
big eyes I can see you." Little Red Riding Hood said: "How
big your hands are!" The beast said: "With my big hands I
can take the bread and the fruit that are in your hands."
Little Red Riding Hood said: "How big your mouth is!" The
beast said: "With my big mouth I can eat the food...and you
too! I regularly eat maidens in the morning." As Little Red
Riding Hood heard these words, she saw that the beast was
not her grandmother. The beast got up from the bed and took
her in its hands and aṭe her. When the beast had eaten
Little Red Riding Hood, it knew that the thing that it had
done was not good. The beast said to itself: "This is not
good! My eyes are bigger than my belly! I am very sick. It
is not good to eat both an old one and a maiden in one day."
And behold, Little Red Riding Hood and her grandmother came
out of the beast's mouth. The beast lay down on the ground,
and Little Red Riding Hood and her grandmother ran to the
city.

Exercise 7 1. הֲלַכְתֶּן 2. דַּעַת 3. לוֹקַחַת 4. תִּהְיֶינָה 5. דַּע

6. שְׁמֹעַ 7. אֵלֵךְ 8. אֶהְיֶה 9. בְּשִׂמְחָה 10. אָמְרָה 11. נִשְׁכַּב

12. פָּעַל, imperfect, 3, m, pl, ב.ש.ח 13. פָּעַל, inf construct

14. פָּעַל, imperative, 2, f, pl, שׁ.מ.ר 14. ל.ק.ה,-,-,-, (with ל)

36

15. פָּעַל, perfect, 3, c, pl, ה.ל.ךְ. 16. פָּעַל, imperfect, 3, m,

ה.י.ה, pl

1. you went 2. know 3. taking 4. they will be 5. know!
6. hear 7. I will go 8. I will be 9. trust! 10. she said
11. we will lie down 12. they will trust 13. to take
14. guard! 15. they went 16. they will be

CHAPTER 20

Exercise 1 1. וַנִּקְצֹר 2. וְגָנַבְתִּי 3. וַתִּלְבַּשׁ 4. וְאָכַל 5. וַיִּזְכְּרוּ

6. וָאֶשְׁמַע 7. וְהָלְכָה 8. וַתִּבְחַרְנָה 9. וָאֶשְׁפֹּט 10. וַיְהִי

11. וְשָׁבַחְתִּי 12. וַאֲמַרְתֶּם 13. וַתִּשְׁמְרִי 14. וַנִּבְטַח 15. וְיָדְעוּ

16. וִישַׁבְתֶּם 17. וַתִּכְתֹּב 18. וָאֶקַּח 19. יִמְלַךְ 20. וּפָתַחְתָּ

21. וַתִּשְׁפַּבְנָה 22. וָאֶשְׁלַח 23. וְזָכַרְנוּ 24. וַתִּקְצֹרְנָה

1. and we harvested 2. and I will steal 3. and she wore
4. and he will eat 5. and they remembered 6. and I heard
7. and she will go 8. and they chose 9. and I judged 10. and
it was or and it came to pass 11. and I will forget
12. and you will say 13. and you guarded 14. and we trusted
15. and they will know 16. and you will settle 17. and you
wrote 18. and I took 19. and he will rule 20. and you will
open 21. and you lay down 22. and I sent 23. and we will
remember 24. and they harvested

Exercise 2 1. A. הֵם שָׁמְעוּ אֶת דִּבְרֵי הַבְּרִית וַיִּזְכְּרוּ אֹתָם וַיִּשְׁמְרוּ

אֹתָם. B. שָׁמַעְתִּי אֶת דִּבְרֵי הַבְּרִית וָאֶזְכֹּר אֹתָם וָאֶשְׁמֹר אֹתָם. C. הַזֶּה

שָׁמְעוּ...וַתִּזְכֹּרְנָה...וַתִּשְׁמֹרְנָה. D. שָׁמַעְתָּ...וַתִּזְכֹּר...וַתִּשְׁמֹר...

E. שָׁמַעְנוּ...וַנִּזְכֹּר...וַנִּשְׁמֹר. F. שָׁמַעְתֶּן...וַתִּזְכֹּרְנָה...וַתִּשְׁמֹרְנָה...

G. שָׁמַעְתָּ...וַתִּזְכְּרִי...וַתִּשְׁמְרִי. H. הוּא שָׁמַע...וַיִּזְכֹּר...וַיִּשְׁמֹר...

I. שָׁמַעְתֶּם...וַתִּזְכְּרוּ...וַתִּשְׁמְרוּ... 2. A. עַתָּה יִקַּח אֶת הַכֵּלִים וְיֵלֵךְ

לְאָהֳלוֹ. B. עַתָּה נִקַּח...וְנֵלֵךְ לְאָהֳלֵנוּ. C. עַתָּה תִּקַּחְנָה...וַתֵּלַכְנָה

לְאָהֳלָן. D. עַתָּה תִּקַּח...וְתֵלֵךְ לְאָהֳלָךְ. E. עַתָּה יִקְחוּ...וְיֵלְכוּ לְאָהֳלָם.

F. עַתָּה תִּקְחִי...וְתֵלְכִי לְאָהֳלֵךְ. 3. A. תִּלְבַּשׁ אֶת בְּגָדֶיךָ וּפְתַחְתֶּם אֶת

37

הַשַּׁעַר וַהֲלַכְתֶּם לְבֵיתְכֶם. B. הוּא יִלְבַּשׁ אֶת בְּגָדָיו וּפָתַח אֶת הַשַּׁעַר וְהָלַךְ
לְבֵיתוֹ. C. תִּלְבַּשְׁנָה אֶת בִּגְדֵיכֶן וּפְתַחְתֶּן אֶת הַשַּׁעַר וַהֲלַכְתֶּן לְבֵיתְכֶן.
D. תִּלְבְּשִׁי אֶת בְּגָדַיִךְ וּפָתַחְתְּ אֶת הַשַּׁעַר וְהָלַכְתְּ לְבֵיתֵךְ. E. הֵנָּה תִּלְבַּשְׁנָה
אֶת בִּגְדֵיהֶן וּפָתְחוּ אֶת הַשַּׁעַר וְהָלְכוּ לְבֵיתָן. F. נִלְבַּשׁ אֶת בְּגָדֵינוּ
וּפָתַחְנוּ אֶת הַשַּׁעַר וְהָלַכְנוּ לְבֵיתֵנוּ. G. הִיא תִּלְבַּשׁ אֶת בְּגָדֶיהָ וּפָתְחָה אֶת
הַשַּׁעַר וְהָלְכָה לְבֵיתָהּ. H. אֶלְבַּשׁ אֶת בְּגָדַי וּפָתַחְתִּי אֶת הַשַּׁעַר וְהָלַכְתִּי
לְבֵיתִי. I. תִּלְבַּשׁ אֶת בְּגָדֶיךָ וּפָתַחְתָּ אֶת הַשַּׁעַר וְהָלַכְתָּ לְבֵיתְךָ.

4. A. תִּהְיוּ מְלָכִים טוֹבִים וּשְׁפַטְתֶּם אֶת עַמְּכֶם. B. הוּא יִהְיֶה מֶלֶךְ טוֹב
וְשָׁפַט אֶת עַמּוֹ. C. הֵם יִהְיוּ מְלָכִים טוֹבִים וְשָׁפְטוּ אֶת עַמָּם. D. אֶהְיֶה
מֶלֶךְ טוֹב וְשָׁפַטְתִּי אֶת עַמִּי. E. נִהְיֶה מְלָכִים טוֹבִים וְשָׁפַטְנוּ אֶת עַמֵּנוּ.

5. A. הִיא יָשְׁבָה עַל אַדְמָתָהּ וַתִּכְתֹּב סֵפֶר לְמִשְׁפַּחְתָּהּ. B. יָשַׁבְתָּ עַל
אַדְמָתְךָ וַתִּכְתָּבְנָה סֵפֶר לְמִשְׁפַּחְתְּכֶן. C. יָשַׁבְתְּ עַל אַדְמָתֵךְ וַתִּכְתְּבִי סֵפֶר
לְמִשְׁפַּחְתֵּךְ. D. יָשַׁבְנוּ עַל אַדְמָתֵנוּ וַנִּכְתֹּב סֵפֶר לְמִשְׁפַּחְתֵּנוּ. E. הֵנָּה יָשְׁבוּ
עַל אַדְמָתָן וַתִּכְתֹּבְנָה סֵפֶר לְמִשְׁפַּחְתָּן. F. יָשַׁבְתָּ עַל אַדְמָתְךָ וַתִּכְתֹּב סֵפֶר
לְמִשְׁפַּחְתְּךָ. G. יְשַׁבְתֶּם עַל אַדְמָתְכֶם וַתִּכְתְּבוּ סֵפֶר לְמִשְׁפַּחְתְּכֶם. H. הֵם יָשְׁבוּ
עַל אַדְמָתָם וַיִּכְתְּבוּ סֵפֶר לְמִשְׁפַּחְתָּם. I. הוּא יָשַׁב עַל אַדְמָתוֹ וַיִּכְתֹּב סֵפֶר
לְמִשְׁפַּחְתּוֹ. 6. A. עַתָּה אַתֶּם בֹּטְחִים בִּבְנְכֶם בְּכָל לְבַבְכֶם. B. עַתָּה אֲנַחְנוּ
בֹּטְחִים בִּבְנֵנוּ בְּכָל לְבָבֵנוּ. C. עַתָּה אַתָּה בֹּטֵחַ בִּבְנְךָ בְּכָל לְבָבְךָ. D. עַתָּה
הֵמָּה בֹּטְחִים בִּבְנָם בְּכָל לְבָבָם. E. עַתָּה בֹּעַז בֹּטֵחַ בִּבְנוֹ בְּכָל לְבָבוֹ.
F. עַתָּה הִיא בֹּטַחַת בִּבְנָהּ בְּכָל לְבָבָהּ. G. עַתָּה אַתְּ בֹּטַחַת בִּבְנֵךְ בְּכָל לְבָבֵךְ.

1. She heard the words of the covenant and she remembered
them and she kept them. A. They heard the words of the
covenant and they remembered them and they kept them. B. I
heard the words...and I remembered...and I kept... C. They
heard...and they remembered...and they kept... D. You heard
...and you remembered...and you kept... E. We heard...and we
remembered...and we kept... F. You heard...and you remembered...and you kept... G. You heard...and you remembered...
and you kept... H. He heard...and he remembered...and he
kept... I. You heard...and you remembered...and you kept...
2. Now I will take the vessels and I will go to my tent.

A. Now he will take the vessels and he will go to his tent.
B. Now we will take...and we will go to our tent. C. Now you
will take...and you will go to your tent. D. Now you will
take...and you will go to your tent. E. Now they will take..
and they will go to their tent. F. Now you will take...and
you will go to your tent. 3. They will put on their clothing
and open the gate and walk to their house. A. You will put
on your clothing and open the gate and walk to your house.
B. He will put on his clothing and open the gate and walk to
his house. C. You will put on your clothing and open the
gate and walk to your house. D. You will put on your
clothing and open the gate and walk to your house. E. They
will put on their clothing and open the gate and walk to
their house. F. We will put on our clothing and open the
gate and walk to our house. G. She will put on her clothing
and open the gate and walk to her house. H. I will put on my
clothing and open the gate and walk to my house. I. You will
put on your clothing and open the gate and walk to your
house. 4. You will be a good king and you will judge your
people. A. You will be good kings and you will judge your
people. B. He will be a good king and he will judge his
people. C. They will be good kings and they will judge their
people. D. I will be a good king and I will judge my people.
E. We will be good kings and we will judge our people. 5. I
stayed upon my land and I wrote a book for my family. A. She
stayed upon her land and she wrote a book for her family.
B. You stayed upon your land and you wrote a book for your
family. C. You stayed upon your land and you wrote a book
for your family. D. We stayed upon our land and we wrote a
book for our family. E. They stayed upon their land and they
wrote a book for their family. F. You stayed upon your land
and you wrote a book for your family. G. You stayed upon
your land and you wrote a book for your family. H. They
stayed upon their land and they wrote a book for their
family. I. He stayed upon his land and he wrote a book for
his family. 6. Now I trust my son with all my heart. A. Now
you trust your son with all your heart. B. Now we trust our
son with all our heart. C. Now you trust your son with all
your heart. D. Now they trust their son with all their heart
E. Now Boaz trusts his son with all his heart. F. Now she
trusts her son with all her heart. G. Now you trust your son
with all your heart.

Exercise 3 1. And it came to pass in the days of the judges
(that) there was a famine in the land. 2. The lad stole all
the money, and he took the money to his brother. 3. We will
remember your kindness, and we will choose you to be king.
4. We ate the bread, and lay down on our beds. 5. We will
send the garment to our father, and he will wear it. 6. The
wise men of Judah knew the words of the covenant, and they
kept them.

Exercise 4a 1. הִיא אָכְלָה מִפְּרִי הָעֵץ וְלָקְחָה מֵהַפְּרִי גַּם לְאִישָׁהּ.

2. דָּוִד בָּטַח בְּדִבְרֵי אָבִיו וּבָחַר בְּאִשָּׁה טוֹבָה לִהְיוֹת לוֹ לְאִשָּׁה. 3. הָלַכְנוּ אֶל רֹאשׁ הָהָר וְשָׁמַעְנוּ אֶת קוֹל הַשּׁוֹפֵט. 4. וְהָיָה אוֹר בַּמִּדְבָּר בַּלַּיְלָה וְהָאֲנָשִׁים יָדְעוּ כִּי אֹהֶל שָׁם.

1. She ate of the fruit of the tree and also gave of the fruit to her husband. 2. David trusted the words of his father and chose a good woman to be a wife for him. 3. We walked to the top of the mountain and heard the voice of the judge. 4. And there was a light in the wilderness, and the people knew that there was a tent there.

Exercise 4b 1. הַנְּעָרִים יִגְנְבוּ אֶת כְּלֵי הַמִּשְׁכָּן וְיִקְחוּ אֹתָם לְאֶרֶץ מוֹאָב.

2. הַזָּקֵן יֵשֵׁב בְּבֵיתוֹ כָּל הַלַּיְלָה וְיִכְתֹּב אֶת סִפְרוֹ עַד הַבֹּקֶר. 3. יִמְלֹךְ הַמֶּלֶךְ עַל כָּל הָאָרֶץ וְיִשְׁפֹּט בְּחֶסֶד. 4. בָּנֶיךָ יִהְיוּ טוֹבִים וְיִזְכְּרוּ אֹתְךָ וְיִבְחֲרוּ לָלֶכֶת בְּדַרְכְּךָ.

1. The young men will steal the vessels of the tabernacle and will take them to the land of Moab. 2. The old man will sit in his house all night and will write his book until the morning. 3. The king will rule over all the land and he will judge with kindness. 4. Your sons will be good and they will remember you and choose to walk in your way.

Exercise 5 1. your land 2. their vessels 3. his silver 4. my life 5. our covenant 6. his heart 7. her soul 8. your stone 9. their tents 10. your heart 11. your dwelling place 12. his mouth 13. your beast 14. our faces 15. their clothing 16. your brothers 17. his head 18. your places 19. my eyes 20. her hands

Exercise 6 In the days of the judges, an old man settled in the land of Israel and his name was Dan. He had animals and fields and houses and only one son, and his name was Joseph. Joseph did not have a wife. So Dan sent a man to the land of his fathers to choose a wife for his son. And the man took in his hand gifts, silver and clothing, and he went to the land of Dan's fathers. In that land there was a woman and her name was Dina. She was not married and she lived in her father's house. The man that Dan had sent went to the house of Dina's family and the man chose Dina as a wife for Joseph. Now Dina's father heard his words and said to himself: "The thing is not good. If Dina goes with the man to the land of Israel, she will not be with her family again all the days of her life." And Dina heard the man's words and she knew that

Dan had animals and fields and houses. And Dina knew that Dan
was a great man. If she went to be a wife to Joseph, she
would have clothes and good food all the days of her life.
And Dina went with the man to the land of Israel and Joseph
took her as a wife for himself. After Joseph took Dina for a
wife, she had clothes and good food and also sons and
daughters.

CHAPTER 21

Exercise 1 1. in you 2. with you 3. in him 4. in them
5. with me 6. to you 7. with them 8. for you 9. in her 10. to
him 11. upon us 12. with us 13. to you 14. in us 15. upon her
16. to me 17. upon you 18. to them 19. from them 20. like me
21. upon you 22. from him/us 23. like her 24.in you 25. to you
26. from you 27. like him 28. for him 29. upon me 30. from
you 31. with us 32. in them 33. like you 34. to them 35. from
her

Exercise 2 1. A. עוֹדְךָ בַּמִּדְבָּר וְאֵינְךָ הוֹלֵךְ מִשָּׁם לַיָּם. B. עוֹדְכֶן...

וְאֵינְכֶן הוֹלְכוֹת...C. עוֹדְנוּ...וְאֵינֶנּוּ הוֹלֵךְ. D. עוֹדִי...וְאֵינֶנִּי

הוֹלֶכֶת...E. עוֹדָם...וְאֵינָם הוֹלְכִים...F. עוֹדְךָ...וְאֵינֵךְ הוֹלֶכֶת...

G. עוֹדְכֶם...וְאֵינְכֶם הוֹלְכִים...H. עוֹדָהּ...וְאֵינֶנָּה הוֹלֶכֶת...I.עוֹדָן

...וְאֵינָן הוֹלְכוֹת...2. A. הֵם יִבְטְחוּ בָנוּ כִּי הֵם זוֹכְרִים אֹתָנוּ.

B. הֵם יִבְטְחוּ בָּךְ כִּי הֵם זוֹכְרִים אֹתָךְ. C. הֵם יִבְטְחוּ בָּם...אֹתָם. D. הֵם

יִבְטְחוּ בּוֹ...אֹתוֹ. E. ...בָּכֶן...אֶתְכֶן. F. ...בְּךָ...אֹתָךְ. G. ...בָּהּ...

...אֹתָהּ. H. ...בָּכֶם...אֶתְכֶם. 3. A. הַמֶּלֶךְ יִקַּח אֶת בָּנַי מִמֶּנִּי וְגָנַב גַּם אֶת

כַּסְפִּי. B. הַמֶּלֶךְ יִקַּח אֶת בְּנֵיהֶ מִמֶּנּוּ...כַּסְפֵּנוּ. C. ...בָּנֶיהָ מִמֶּנָּה

כַּסְפָּהּ. D. ...בָּנַיִךְ מִמֵּךְ...כַּסְפֵּךְ. E. ...בְּנֵיהֶם מֵהֶם...כַּסְפָּם.

F. ...בָּנָיו מִמֶּנּוּ...כַּסְפּוֹ. G. ...בָּנֶיהָ מִמֶּנָּה...כַּסְפָּהּ. H. ...בְּנֵיהֶן

מֵהֶן...כַּסְפָּן. I. ...בְּנֵיהֶ מֵהֶם...כַּסְפָּהּ. 4. A. עָלֵינוּ לִבְחֹר נָשִׁים

חֲכָמוֹת לִשְׁמֹר אֶת בְּנוֹתֵינוּ. B. עָלַיִךְ...בְּנוֹתַיִךְ. C. עֲלֵיכֶם...בְּנוֹתֵיכֶם.

D. עֲלֵיהֶן...בְּנוֹתֵיהֶן. E. עָלַי...בְּנוֹתַי. F. עָלָיו...בְּנוֹתָיו.

G. עָלַיִךְ...בְּנוֹתַיִךְ. 5. A. הִנֵּה הֹלְכִי אֵלֵינוּ לָשֶׁבֶת עִמָּנוּ וַתִּשְׁמַעְנָה

41

בְּקוֹלֵנוּ וַתִּשְׁמֹרְנָה אֹתָנוּ. B. הֵנָּה הָלְכוּ אֲלֵיהֶם לָשֶׁבֶת עִמָּהֶם וַתִּשְׁמַעְנָה

בְּקוֹלָם וַתִּשְׁמֹרְנָה אֹתָם. C. ...אֵלַי...עִמִּי...בְּקוֹלִי...אֹתִי... D. ...אֵלֶיהָ

עִמָּהּ...בְּקוֹלָהּ...אֹתָהּ... E. ...אֲלֵיכֶן...עִמָּכֶן...בְּקוֹלְכֶן...אֶתְכֶן.

...אֵלָיו...עִמּוֹ...בְּקוֹלוֹ...אֹתוֹ... G. ...אֲלֵיכֶם...עִמָּכֶם...בְּקוֹלְכֶם. F

...אֶתְכֶם. H. ...אֵלֶיךָ...עִמְּךָ...בְּקוֹלְךָ...אֹתָךְ.

1. We are still in the wilderness and we are not going from there to the sea. A. You are still in the wilderness and you are not going from there to the sea. B. You are still...and you are not going... C. He is still...and he is not going... D. I am still...and I am not going... E. They are still...and they are not going... F. You are still...and you are not going... G. You are still...and you are not going... H. She is still...and she is not going... I. They are still...and they are not going... 2. They will trust me because they remember me. A. They will trust us because they remember us. B. They will trust you because they remember you. C. They will trust them...remember them. D. ...trust him...remember him. E. ...trust you...remember you. F. ...trust you... remember you. G. ...trust her...remember her. H. ...trust you ...remember you. 3. The king will take your sons from you and also steal your money. A. The king will take my sons from me and also steal my money. B. ...our sons from us...our money. C. ...her sons from her...her money. D. ...your sons from you ...your money. E. ...their sons from them...their money. F. ...his sons from him...his money. G. ...your sons from you ...your money. H. ...their sons from them...their money. I. ...your sons from you...your money. 4. She must choose wise women to guard her daughters. A. We must choose wise women to guard our daughters. B. You must choose...your daughters. C. You must choose...your daughers. D. They must choose...their daughters. E. I must choose...my daughters. F. He must choose...his daughters. G. You must choose...your daughters. 5. They went to you to stay with you and they obeyed you and guarded you. A. They went to us to stay with us and they obeyed us and guarded us. B. They went to them to stay with them and they obeyed them and guarded them. C. They went to me to stay with me and they obeyed me and guarded me. D. They went to her to stay with her and they obeyed her and guarded her. E. They went to you to stay with you and they obeyed you and guarded you. F. They went to him to stay with him and they obeyed him and guarded him. G. They went to you to stay with you and they obeyed you and guarded you. H. They went to you to stay with you and they obeyed you and guarded you.

Exercise 3 .2 תֵּלְכִי עִמָּנוּ עַד הָעִיר. .3 הוּא יִגְנֹב מִמֶּנִּי אֶת הַכֹּל.

.4 נִבְחַר בְּךָ מִכָּל הַנְּעָרִים. .5 הֵם יֵלְכוּ אַחֲרַיִךְ בַּדֶּרֶךְ לְבֵית לֶחֶם.

1. Now she must write to her mother. 2. You will go with us
as far as the city. 3. He will steal everything from me.
4. We will choose you from all the young men. 5. They will go
after you on the road to Bethlehem.

Exercise 4a .1 אֵינֶנִּי .2 אֵינֶנּוּ .3 אֵינָן .4 אֵינֶנָּה

1. I am not in the tent with them. 2. We are not in the darkness with the beasts in the wilderness. 3. They are not
eating the fruit. 4. She does not remember the face of her
husband.

Exercise 4b .1 עוֹדְכֶם .2 עוֹדֶנִּי .3 עוֹדֵנוּ – עוֹדֶנּוּ .4 עוֹדָם

1. You are still good men. 2. I still know these things.
3. We are/He is still with the holy ones in the tabernacle.
4. They are still lying down in their tents today.

Exercise 5 .1 מִמֶּנָּה .2 כָּמוֹנִי .3 בּוֹ .4 עָלֵינוּ .5 עִמָּךְ

1. The men went to the maiden's house and they stole money
from her. 2. Like me, you are from the family of Jacob. 3. We
will trust in him and we will remember his words. 4. He sat
upon his throne and ruled over us. 5. They chose you and they
went with you.

Exercise 6 .1 עוֹדֶנִּי עַל אַדְמָתִי. .2 עוֹדְךָ עַל אַדְמָתְךָ. .3 עוֹדֶנוּ

עַל אַדְמָתֵנוּ. .4 הִיא יוֹשֶׁבֶת עִמָּנוּ. .5 אֲנִי יוֹשֶׁבֶת עִמָּהֶם. .6 אַתֶּן

יוֹשְׁבוֹת עִמּוֹ. .7 אֵינָם כָּמוֹנִי. .8 אֵינֶךָ כָּמוֹהֶן. .9 הָלַכְתִּי לְבֵיתִי

עִם אִמִּי וְיָשַׁבְתִּי שָׁם. .10 הָלַכְתָּ לְבֵיתְךָ עִם אִמְּךָ וְיָשַׁבְתָּ בְּכִסְאֶךָ.

.11 הוּא הָלַךְ לְבֵיתוֹ הַגָּדוֹל עִם אִמּוֹ הַזְּקֵנָה וְאָבִיו הַזָּקֵן. .12 הָלַכְנוּ

לְבֵית אִמֵּנוּ הַגָּדוֹל כַּאֲשֶׁר הִיא הָיְתָה שָׁם.

CHAPTER 22

Exercise 2 .1 A. הוּא רָאָה אֶת הַמִּשְׁכָּן אֲשֶׁר בְּנֵי יִשְׂרָאֵל בָּנוּ בַּמִּדְבָּר.

B. רָאִיתָ אֶת הַמִּשְׁכָּן... C. הַקּוֹצְרִים רָאוּ... D. רְאִיתֶן... E. רָאִיתִי...

43

Chapter 22

F. ...רָאִיתָ. G. ...שָׂרָה רָאֲתָה. H. הִנֵּה רָאוּ... I. ...רְאִיתֶם...

2. A. בֵּין הָעַרְבַּיִם שָׁתִיתִי יַיִן מֵהֲפָלִי. B. בֵּין הָעַרְבַּיִם שָׁתִיתָ...

C. ...הִנֵּה שָׁתוּ... D. ...הוּא שָׁתָה... E. ...שָׁתִית... F. ..שָׁתִינוּ.

... G. ...הֵמָּה שָׁתוּ... H. ...שָׁתִיתֶן... I. ...שָׁתִיתְ... 3. A. עָלִי

עַל הָאֲדָמָה לִבְנוֹת אֶת בָּתַּיִךְ. B. עֲלִינָה...בָּתֵּיכֶן. C. עֲלוּ...בָּתֵּיכֶם.

D. עֲלֵה...בָּתֶּיהָ. E. עֲלִינָה...בָּתֵּיכֶן. 4. A. תִּרְאֶינָה זָקֵן אֲשֶׁר הֹלֵךְ

בַּדֶּרֶךְ וּבְטַחְתֶּן בּוֹ וּפְתַחְתֶּן לוֹ אֶת שַׁעֲרֵי עִירְכֶן. B. נִרְאֶה...וּבָטַחְנוּ בּוֹ

וּפָתַחְנוּ...עִירֵנוּ. C. הוּא יִרְאֶה...וּבָטַח בּוֹ וּפָתַח...עִירוֹ. D. הֵמָּה

יִרְאוּ...וּבָטְחוּ בּוֹ וּפָתְחוּ...עִירָם. E. תִּרְאִי...וּבָטַחְתְּ בּוֹ וּפָתַחְתְּ...

עִירֵךְ. F. הִיא תִּרְאֶה...וּבָטְחָה בּוֹ וּפָתְחָה...עִירָהּ. G. תִּרְאוּ...וּבְטַחְתֶּם

בּוֹ וּפְתַחְתֶּם...עִירְכֶם. H. הִנֵּה תִּרְאֶינָה...וּבָטְחוּ בּוֹ וּפָתְחוּ...עִירָן.

I. אֶרְאֶה...וּבָטַחְתִּי בּוֹ וּפָתַחְתִּי...עִירִי. 5. A. הָאִישׁ הַקָּדוֹשׁ אָמַר אֵלַי

"תַּעֲשֶׂה חֶסֶד כַּאֲבוֹתֶיךָ" וְשָׁמַעְתִּי בְּקוֹלוֹ. B. ...אֵלַיִךְ "תַּעֲשֶׂה חֶסֶד

כַּאֲבוֹתֶיהָ" וְשָׁמְעָה בְּקוֹלוֹ. C. ...אֲלֵיכֶן "תַּעֲשֶׂינָה חֶסֶד כַּאֲבוֹתֵיכֶן"

וּשְׁמַעְתֶּן בְּקוֹלוֹ. D. ...אֲלֵיהֶם "תַּעֲשׂוּ חֶסֶד כַּאֲבוֹתֵיכֶם" וְשָׁמְעוּ בְּקוֹלוֹ.

E. ...אֵלַיִךְ "תַּעֲשִׂי חֶסֶד כַּאֲבוֹתַיִךְ" וְשָׁמַעְתְּ בְּקוֹלוֹ. F. ...אֲלֵיהֶן

"תַּעֲשֶׂינָה חֶסֶד כַּאֲבוֹתֵיכֶן" וְשָׁמְעוּ בְּקוֹלוֹ. G. ...אֵלָיו "תַּעֲשֶׂי חֶסֶד

כַּאֲבוֹתָיו" וְשָׁמְעָה בְּקוֹלוֹ. H. ...אֲלֵיכֶם "תַּעֲשׂוּ חֶסֶד כַּאֲבוֹתֵיכֶם" וּשְׁמַעְתֶּם

בְּקוֹלוֹ.

1. We saw the tabernacle that the children of Israel built in the wilderness. A. He saw the tabernacle that the children of Israel built in the wilderness. B. You saw... C. The harvesters saw... D. You saw... E. I saw... F. You saw... G. Sarah saw... H. They saw... I. You saw... 2. At dusk, she drank wine from the vessel. A. At dusk, I drank wine from the vessel. B. At dusk, you drank... C. At dusk, they drank... D. At dusk, he drank... E. At dusk, you drank... F. At dusk, we drank... G. At dusk, they drank... H. At dusk, you drank... I. At dusk, you drank... 3. Go up upon the land to build your houses. A. Go up upon the land to build your houses! B. Go up ...your houses! C. You and David, go up...your houses! D. Go up...your houses! E. You and Naomi, go up...your houses!

4. You will see an old man who is walking on the road and you
will trust him and open the gates of your city for him.
A. You will see an old man who is walking on the road and you
will trust him and open the gates of your city for him. B. We
will see...and we will trust him and open...our city... C. He
will see...and he will trust him and open...his city...
D. They will see...and they will trust him and open...their
city... E. You will see...and you will trust him and open...
your city... F. She will see...and she will trust him and
open...her city... G. You will see...and you will trust him
and open...your city... H. They will see...and they will
trust him and open...their city... I. I will see...and I will
trust him and open...my city... 5. The holy man said to us,
"You will do kindness like your fathers" and we obeyed him.
A. The holy man said to me, "You will do kindness like your
fathers" and I obeyed him. B. ...to you, "You will do
kindness like your fathers" and you obeyed him. C. ...you,
"You will do kindness like your fathers" and you obeyed him.
D. ...them, "You will do kindness like your fathers" and they
obeyed him. E. ...you, "You will do kindness like your
fathers" and you obeyed him. F. ...them, "You will do kindness like your fathers" and they obeyed him. G. ...her, "You
will do kindness like your fathers" and she obeyed him.
H. ...you, "You will do kindness like your fathers" and you
obeyed him.

Exercise 3 1. עוֹנֶה 2. תַּעֲלוּ 3. לִבְנוֹת 4. רְאֵה 5. עֲשֹׂה יַעֲשׂוּ

1. You say "All that is under the heavens is evil" and I
answer you "No". 2. You will go up with me in the evening
from the sea as far as the mountains of Jerusalem. 3. I will
choose these people to build my house. 4. See these words
that are written and do not forget them. 5. They will surely
do all that their fathers did.

Exercise 4 1. עָלָה, עוֹלֶה, יַעֲלֶה, עָלֹה עָלָה, עָלֹה יַעֲלֶה 2. שְׁתִי
3. עֲשִׂיתֶם, עוֹשִׂים, תַּעֲשִׂי, עָשֹׂה עֲשִׂיתֶם, עָשֹׂה תַּעֲשֶׂה, עֲשׂוּ 4. עָנָה
5. בָּנִינוּ, בּוֹנִים, נִבְנֶה, בָּנֹה בָּנִינוּ, בָּנֹה נִבְנֶה 6. תִּשְׁתֶּה 7. רְאִיתֶן
רוֹאוֹת, תִּרְאֶינָה, רָאֹה רְאִיתֶן, רָאֹה תִּרְאֶינָה, רְאֶינָה

1. All this nation (went up, is going up, will go up, surely
went up, will surely go up) from the wilderness to the land
of Israel. 2. Sit with your family in the field and (drink!)
only the water! 3. You (did, are doing, will do, surely did,
will surely do, do!) evil in the eyes of the judge. 4. I said
to him: "Behold, bread and water and fruit" and he (answered)
"I will remember your kindness". 5. We (built, are building,
will build, surely built, will surely build) the gates of our

45

city. 6. When you go to Moab, don't (drink) the water.
7. You (saw, are seeing, will see, surely saw, will surely
see, see!) the lad's face regularly.

Exercise 5 1. We ate the food and drank water and sat in
our tent at dusk. 2. The man went up to Jerusalem and saw
his uncle there. 3. And it was dark, and the women went to
their house. 4. They must build a city in the midst of the
wilderness, and they will build it.

Shortened Verbs: 1. וַנֵּשֶׁב 2. וַיֵּרֶא 3. וַיְהִי

Exercise 6 1. פ.ת.ח 2. ה.ל.ך 3. ל.ק.ח 4. ב.נ.ה 5. שׁ.כ.ח.

6. ר.א.ה 7. ה.י.ה 8. ע.שׂ.ה 9. ע.נ.ה 10. שׁ.ת.ה 11. ה.ל.ך.

12. ה.י.ה 13. ב.נ.ה 14. ל.ק.ח 15. ר.א.ה 16. שׁ.ת.ה.

17. ע.נ.ה 18. ע.שׂ.ה

1. I opened 2. go! 3.you will take 4. you built 5. and
I forgot 6. and she saw/you saw 7. be 8. and we did
9. to answer 10. drinking 11. I will go 12. and it was -
and it came to pass 13. and you/she built 14. take!
15. see! 16. and I drank 17. we answered 18. do!

Exercise 8 1. כָּתַבְתִּי 2. בָּנִיתִי 3. עָלִיתִי 4. שָׁתִיתֶם 5. שְׁמַרְתֶּם

6. עֲשִׂיתֶם 7. יִשְׁפֹּט 8. יִרְאֶה 9. עָשָׂה 10. הָיָה 11. עוֹשֶׂה

12. כּוֹתֵבְת 13. יְשַׁבְתָּן 14. עָלִיתֶן

1. I wrote 2. I built 3. I went up 4. you drank 5. you
guarded 6. you did 7. he will judge 8. he will see 9. he did
10. he was 11. doing 12. writing 13. you sat 14. you went up

CHAPTER 23

Exercise 2 1. A. הִיא קָמָה בַּבֹּקֶר וַתִּשְׁכַּב בָּעֶרֶב. B. קַמְתֶּן...

C. קַמְנוּ...וַנִּשְׁכַּב... D. קַמְתְּ...וַתִּשְׁכְּבִי... E. הוּא וַתִּשְׁכַּבְנָה

קָם...וַיִּשְׁכַּב... F. הֵנָּה קָמוּ...וַתִּשְׁכַּבְנָה... G. קַמְתֶּם...וַתִּשְׁכְּבוּ...

H. קַמְתְּ...וַתִּשְׁכַּב I. הֵם קָמוּ...וַיִּשְׁכְּבוּ 2.A. סָתוּר אֶשֶׁת בֹּעַז מֵהַדֶּרֶךְ וְרָצָה

לָקַחַת אֶת הָאֹכֶל מֵהָאֹהֶל. B. נָסוּר מֵהַדֶּרֶךְ וְרַצְנוּ... C. הַנְּעָרִים יָסוּרוּ

D. ...סָתוּרוּ...וְרָצְתֶם... E. תָּסֹרְנָה נְשֵׁי יְרוּשָׁלַם...וְרָצוּ

46

F. תָּסוּר...וְרַצְתָּ...‏ G. תָּסוּרִי...וְרַצְתְּ...‏ H. תָּסוּרֶינָה...וְרַצְתֶּן...‏

I. אָסוּר...וְרַצְתִּי...‏ 3. A. קַמְנוּ וּבָאנוּ אֶל הָאִישׁ הַקָּדוֹשׁ לִשְׁמֹעַ אֶת

דְּבָרָיו. B. הוּא יָקוּם וְיָבוֹא...‏ C. קַמְתֶּם וּבָאתֶם...‏ D. אָקוּם

וְאָבוֹא...‏ E. תָּקוּמִי וְתָבוֹאִי...‏ 4. A. בְּשׁוּב הָאִישׁ מֵהַשָּׂדֶה אֶל בֵּיתוֹ

יָשַׁב וְאָכַל וְשָׁתָה וְשָׂר. B. בְּשׁוּבִי מֵהַשָּׂדֶה אֶל בֵּיתִי יָשַׁבְתִּי וְאָכַלְתִּי

שָׁתִיתִי וְשָׂרְתִּי. C. בְּשׁוּבְכֶם...בָּתֵּיכֶם יְשַׁבְתֶּם וַאֲכַלְתֶּם וּשְׁתִיתֶם וְשָׂרְתֶּם.

D. בְּשׁוּבֵךְ...בֵּיתֵךְ יָשַׁבְתְּ וְאָכַלְתְּ וְשָׁתִית וְשָׂרְתְּ. E. בְּשׁוּב הַנְּשִׁים...‏

בָּתֵּיהֶם יָשְׁבוּ וְאָכְלוּ וְשָׁתוּ וְשָׂרוּ. F. בְּשׁוּבֵנוּ...בָּתֵּינוּ יָשַׁבְנוּ וְאָכַלְנוּ

וְשָׁתִינוּ וְשָׂרְנוּ. G. בְּשׁוּבָהּ...בֵּיתָהּ יָשְׁבָה וְאָכְלָה וְשָׁתְתָה וְשָׂרָה.

H. בְּשׁוּבְכֶן...בָּתֵּיכֶן יְשַׁבְתֶּן וַאֲכַלְתֶּן וּשְׁתִיתֶן וְשָׂרְתֶּן. I. בְּשׁוּבְךָ...‏

בֵּיתְךָ יָשַׁבְתָּ וְאָכַלְתָּ וְשָׁתִית וְשָׂרְתָּ. 5. A. הוּא יָשִׂים לְפָנָיו מְנָחוֹת וְכֶסֶף

שָׁנָה בְּשָׁנָה וְהוּא יִשְׁמֹר אֹתוֹ מִכָּל רָע. B. תָּשִׂימוּ...וְהוּא יִשְׁמֹר אֶתְכֶם...‏

C. הֵנָּה תְּשִׂימֶינָה...אֹתָן...‏ D. תָּשִׂים...אֹתָךְ. E. ...אָשִׂים...אֹתִי...‏

F. תְּשֵׂמְנָה...אֶתְכֶן...‏ G. הִיא תָּשִׂים...אֹתָהּ...‏ H. תָּשִׂימִי...אֹתָךְ...‏

I. הֵמָּה יָשִׂימוּ...אֹתָם...‏

1. I arose in the morning and lay down in the evening.
A. She arose in the morning and lay down in the evening.
B. You arose...and lay down... C. We arose...and lay down...
D. You arose...and lay down... E. He arose...and lay down...
F. They arose...and lay down... G. You arose...and lay down
... H. You arose...and lay down... I. They arose...and lay
down... 2. The man will turn aside from the road and he will
run to take the food from the tent. A. Boaz's wife will turn
aside from the road and she will run to take the food from
the tent. B. We will turn aside...and we will run... C. The
lads will turn aside...and they will run... D. You will turn
aside...and you will run... E. The women of Jerusalem will
turn aside...and they will run... F. You will turn aside...
and you will run... G. You will turn aside...and you will
run... H. You will turn aside...and you will run... I. I
will turn aside...and I will run... 3. I arose and went to
the holy man to hear his words. A. We arose and went to the
holy man to hear his words. B. He will arise and will go...
C. You arose and went...D. I will arise and will go...E.You
will arise and will go...4.When the harvesters returned from

47

the field to their houses, they sat and ate and drank and
sang. A. When the man returned from the field to his house,
he sat and ate and drank and sang. B. When I returned from
the field to my house, I sat and ate and drank and sang.
C. When you returned from the field to your houses, you sat
and ate and drank and sang. D. When you returned from the
field to your house, you sat and ate and drank and sang.
E. When the women returned...their houses, they sat and ate
and drank and sang. F. When we returned...our houses, we sat
and ate and drank and sang. G. When she returned...her house
she sat and ate and drank and sang. H. When you returned...
your houses, you sat and ate and drank and sang. I. When you
returned...your house, you sat and ate and drank and sang.
5. We will set gifts and silver before him year by year and
he will guard us from all evil. A. He will set gifts and
silver before him year by year and he will guard him from
all evil. B. You will set....and he will guard you...
C. They will set...and he will guard them... D. You will set
...and he will guard you... E. I will set...and he will
guard me... F. You will set...and he will guard you...
G. She will set...and he will guard her... H. You will set..
and he will guard you... I. They will set...and he will
guard you...

Exercise 3 .1 בָּאוּ, בָּאִים, יָבוֹאוּ, בּוֹא בָּאוּ, בּוֹא יָבוֹאוּ .2 סוּרִי

.3 קַמְנוּ, קָמִים, נָקוּם, קוֹם קַמְנוּ, קוֹם נָקוּם .4 שָׁם, שָׁם, יָשִׂים,

שׂוֹם שָׂם, שׂוֹם יָשִׂים .5 רַצְתִּי, רָץ, אָרוּץ, רוֹץ רַצְתִּי, רוֹץ אָרוּץ

.6 שָׁרָה, שָׁרָה, תָּשִׁיר, שׁוֹר שָׁרָה, שׁוֹר תָּשִׁיר

1. They (came, are coming, will come, surely came, will
surely come) to harvest daily. 2. (Turn aside!) from evil
and go the good way. 3. We (arose, are arising, will arise,
surely arose, will surely arise) to go up on the mountain.
4. He (paid attention, is paying attention, will pay attention, paid close attention, will pay close attention) to his
mother's voice. 5. When my brothers return(ed) to their land
I (ran, run, will run, surely ran, will surely run) to see
them. 5. She regularly (sang, sings, will sing, really sang
will really sing) in the evening with her family.

Exercise 4a .1 תָּשִׂימוּ .2 יָשׁוּב, וְיִבְנֶה .3 יָסוּרוּ, וְיַעֲשׂוּ

.4 נֹאכַל, וְנִשְׁתֶּה, וְנָקוּם

1. You will set the words of the covenant upon your hearts
and upon your souls. 2. He will return to his land and build
there a house from stone. 3.They will turn aside from the
covenant and do evil in the eyes of their fathers. 4. We

will eat and drink and arise to go to our tents.

Exercise 4b 1. עָשִׂינוּ, וְשַׂמְנוּ 2. עָנוּ, בָּאנוּ 3. שָׁבָה 4. שָׁרַתֶּן

1. We made vessels of silver and we put them in the tabernacle. 2. They answered, "We came to see you". 3. She
returned to her father's house year by year. 4. You sang
with all the people of the city.

Exercise 5   1. The old man went and came to the holy
mountain and went up upon it. 2. You heard the sound of a
beast and saw it and turned aside from the road. 3. And Ruth
returned with Naomi to the land of Israel and settled with
her there. 4. And he built a chair for himself from wood,
and he put the money under it and he sat upon it. 5. And it
came to pass in the morning that the maiden arose from her
bed and put on her clothing and went to the house of her
brother. 6. I will pay attention to the words of the wise,
and I will turn aside from evil.

Shortened Verbs: 1. וַיַּעַל 2. וַתֵּרֶא, וַתָּסַר 3. וַתֵּשֶׁב 4. וַיִּבֶן,
5. וַיָּשֶׂם וַיְהִי, וַתָּקָם

Exercise 6   There was a man who lived in a tent in the
desert. He had sons and daughters, but he had no money. And
the day came when there was no food for his family...

Exercise 7 1. שַׁבְתָּ 2. עָשִׂיתָ 3. זָכַרְתָּ 4. בָּאתָ 5. נָרוּץ
6. נַעֲלֶה 7. נָסוּר 8. נִשְׁמֹר 9. בָּאָה 10. בּוֹנָה 11. בָּאָה
12. כָּתְבָה 13. הָיְתָה 14. תִּהְיֶינָה 15. תָּקֹמְנָה/תְּקוּמֶינָה 16. יָשִׁירוּ
17. שַׂמְתָּ 18. שִׁיר 19. קוּמִי 20. אָקוּם 21. אָבוֹא

1. you returned 2. you did 3. you remembered 4. you went
5. we will run 6. we will go up 7. we will turn aside 8. we
will guard 9. coming 10. building 11. she came 12. she wrote
13. she was 14. they will be 15. they will get up 16. they
will sing 17. you put 18. sing! 19. get up! 20. I will get
up 21. I will come

CHAPTER 24

Exercise 2 1. A. הוּא אָמַר בְּלִבּוֹ: "אָסוּר מִמַּעֲשֵׂי הָרָעִים." B. הוּא
אָמַר בְּלִבּוֹ: "הִיא תָּסוּר מִמַּעֲשֶׂיהָ הָרָעִים." C. ..."הוּא יָסוּר מִמַּעֲשָׂיו

49

הָרֵעִים." D. ..."הִנֵּה תָּסֹרְנָה מִמַּעֲשֵׂיהֶן הָרָעִים." E. ..."בָּנַי יָסוּרוּ

מִמַּעֲשֵׂיהֶם הָרָעִים." 2. A. תִּתְּנוּ לָהֶם מַיִם מֵהַיַּרְדֵּן בָּעֶרֶב וְהֵם יִשְׁתּוּ אֹתָם.

B. הִנֵּה תִּתֵּנָה ...C. אֶתֵּן ...D. הוּא יִתֵּן ...E. תִּתְּנִי ...F. הֵמָּה

יִתְּנוּ ...G. תִּתֵּנָה ...H. תִּתֵּן ...I. נִתֵּן ...3. A. וַיֹּאמֶר דָּוִד

אֶל אִמּוֹ לֵאמֹר: "אַבְרָהָם יֹאכַל אֶת הַפְּרִי." B. ..."הַבָּנִים יֹאכְלוּ..."

C. ..."הַנְּעָרוֹת תֹּאכַלְנָה..." D. ..."בַּתִּי תֹּאכַל..." E. ..."נֹאכַל.."

F. ..."אַנְשֵׁי מִצְרַיִם יֹאכְלוּ..." G. ..."תֹּאכְלִי..." 4. A. הִיא

תֶּאֱהַב אֶת מַלְכָּהּ בְּכָל לִבָּהּ וְתַעֲשֶׂה מַעֲשִׂים רַבִּים בִּשְׁמוֹ. B. תֶּאֱהַבְנָה אֶת

מַלְכְּכֶן בְּכָל לִבְּכֶן וְתַעֲשֶׂינָה ...C. הֵמָּה יֶאֱהֲבוּ אֶת מַלְכָּם בְּכָל לִבָּם

וְיַעֲשׂוּ ...D. נֶאֱהַב אֶת מַלְכֵּנוּ בְּכָל לִבֵּנוּ וְנַעֲשֶׂה ...E. הוּא יֶאֱהַב אֶת

מַלְכּוֹ בְּכָל לִבּוֹ וְיַעֲשֶׂה ...F. תֶּאֱהֲבִי אֶת מַלְכֵּךְ בְּכָל לִבֵּךְ וְתַעֲשִׂי...

G. אֹהַב אֶת מַלְכִּי בְּכָל לִבִּי וְאֶעֱשֶׂה ...H. הֵנָּה תֶּאֱהַבְנָה אֶת מַלְכָּן בְּכָל

לִבָּן וְתַעֲשֶׂינָה ...I. תֶּאֱהֲבוּ אֶת מַלְכְּכֶם בְּכָל לִבְּכֶם וְתַעֲשׂוּ...

5. A. נָתַתְּ לַזָּקֵן אֶת הַלֶּחֶם וְאֶת הַיַּיִן. B. הוּא נָתַן ...C. נְתַתֶּן...

D. הֵמָּה נָתְנוּ ...E. הִיא נָתְנָה ...F. נָתַתָּ ...G. נָתַתִּי ...H. הֵנָּה

נָתְנוּ ...I. נְתַתֶּם ...6. A. שָׂרָה לָקְחָה אֶת סִפְרֵי הַתּוֹרָה וַתִּתֵּן אֹתָם

לְבָנֶיהָ. B. הַנָּשִׁים לָקְחוּ...וַתִּתֵּנָּה אֹתָם לִבְנֵיהֶן. C. לָקַחְתִּי...וָאֶתֵּן

אֹתָם לְבָנַי. D. לָקַחְתָּ...וַתִּתֵּנִי אֹתָם לְבָנֶיךָ. E. לְקַחְתֶּם...וַתִּתְּנוּ אֹתָם

לִבְנֵיכֶם. F. לָקַחְנוּ...וַנִּתֵּן אֹתָם לְבָנֵינוּ. G. הָאֲנָשִׁים לָקְחוּ...וַיִּתְּנוּ

אֹתָם לִבְנֵיהֶם. H. לְקַחְתֶּן...וַתִּתֵּנָּה אֹתָם לִבְנֵיכֶן. I. לָקַחְתְּ...וַתִּתֵּן

אֹתָם לְבָנַיִךְ.

1. He said to himself: "They will turn aside from their evil deeds." A. He said to himself: "I will turn aside from my evil deeds." B. .."She will turn aside from her evil deeds." C. ..."He will turn aside from his evil deeds." D. ..."They will turn aside from their evil deeds." E. ..."My sons will turn aside from their evil deeds." 2. She will give water from the Jordan to them in the evening and they will drink it. A. You will give water from the Jordan to them in the evening and they will drink it. B. They will give water...

C. I will give... D. He will give... E. You will give...
F. They will give... G. You will give... H. You will give...
I. We will give..3.And David said to his mother, saying, "I
will eat the fruit." A.And David said to his mother, saying,
"Abraham will eat the fruit." B. ..."The sons will eat..."
C. ..."The maidens will eat..." D. ..."Your daughter will
eat..." E. ..."We will eat..." F. ..."The people of Egypt
will eat..." G. ..."You will eat..." 4. You will love your
king with all your heart and you will do many deeds in his
name. A. She will love her king with all her heart and she
will do many deeds in his name. B. You will love your king
with all your heart and you will do... C. They will love
their king with all their heart and they will do... D. We
will love our king with all our heart and we will do...
E. He will love his king with all his heart and he will do..
F. You will love your king with all your heart and you will
do... G. I will love my king with all my heart and I will
do... H. They will love their king with all their heart and
they will do... I. You will love your king with all your
heart and you will do... 5. We gave the bread and the wine
to the old man. A. You gave the bread and the wine to the
old man. B. He gave... C. You gave... D. They gave... E. She
gave... F. You gave... G. I gave... H. They gave... I. You
gave... 6. He took the books of the law and he gave them to
his sons. A. Sarah took the books of the law and she gave
them to her sons. B. The women took...and they gave them to
their sons. C. I took...and I gave them to my sons. D. You
took...and you gave them to your sons... E. You took...and
you gave them to your sons. F. We took...and we gave them to
our sons. G. The people took...and they gave them to their
sons. H. You took...and you gave them to your sons. I. You
took...and you gave them to your sons.

Exercise 3 1. נָתַן, נוֹתֵן, יִתֵּן, נָחוֹן נָתַן, נָחוֹן יִתֵּן 2. אֲהַבְתֶּם,

אוֹהֲבִים, תֶּאֱהַבוּ, אָהוֹב אֲהַבְתֶּם, אָהוֹב תֶּאֱהַבוּ, אֱהַב 3. תֹּאכְלִי

4. עָשִׂיתִי, עוֹשֶׂה, אֶעֱשֶׂה, עָשֹׂה עָשִׂיתִי, עָשֹׂה אֶעֱשֶׂה 5. אָמַרְתְּ, אוֹמֶרֶת,

תֹּאמְרִי, אָמוֹר אָמַרְתְּ, אָמוֹר תֹּאמְרִי, אִמְרִי

1. He (gave, is giving, will give, surely gave, will surely
give) many vessels to his wife. 2. You (loved, love, will
love, really love, will really love, love!) the truth and
your mother's food. 3. Week by week, you will come to my
house and (you will eat) my food. 4. I (did, am doing, will
do, certainly did, will·certainly do) deeds of kindness and
compassion daily, because I am better than all the people of
my city. 5. You (said, are saying, will say, surely said,
will surely say) to your daughters, saying, "You have heard
only words of truth from the mouth of your mother."

Exercise 4 1. אֶל יְרוּשָׁלַם 2. עַל הָהָר 3. שָׁם 4. אֶל הָעִיר

5. אֶל הָאָרֶץ

1. Next week, the lads will run to Jerusalem to give their fathers much money. 2. Jacob went up on the mountain to forget the love of money. 3. And the old man said to them, "Go there to do deeds of kindness and compassion." 4. And the king sent the judge to the city and said to him, "Pay attention to the deeds of my people, and judge them with kindness." 5. We must return to the land after the famine.

Exercise 5 יָשְׁבָה, אָהֲבוּ, בָּאוּ, רְאוֹת, שָׁמָה, לְכִי, סוּרִי, שׁוּבוּ,

שִׁמְעוּ, הָלְכוּ, שָׁב, אָמַר, אוֹהֵב, אֶתֵּן, אוּכַל, לָתֵת, רָאֲתָה, אָהֲבָה, הָיְתָה

There was a woman who lived in the land of Canaan and her name was Sarah. There were many men who loved her. They came daily to see her, but she did not pay attention to their words. Sarah said to them: "Go! Turn aside from me and return to your houses!" They obeyed her and went on their way. One man returned to her house every week. He said to her: "I love you with all my heart! I will give you everything that I can give!" Sarah saw that he was a good man. She loved him and became his wife.

Exercise 6 1. א.ה.ב 2. כ.ת.ב 3. א.ה.ב 4. ק.ר.ם

5. נ.ת.ן 6. שׁ.י.ם 7. ב.ח.ר 8. ע.נ.ה 9. א.מ.ר 10. י.שׁ.ב

11. ב.ו.א 12. א.מ.ר 13. נ.ת.ן 14. י.שׁ.ב 15. שׁ.י.ם

16. ע.נ.ה 17. כ.ת.ב 18. ב.ו.א 19. ב.ח.ר 20. נ.ת.ן

1. we loved 2. I will write 3. loving 4. arise! 5. you gave 6. set! 7. choosing 8. we answered 9. you will say 10. to sit 11. he came or coming 12. saying 13. you/she will give 14. you sat 15. we will put 16. answering 17. you/they will write 18. come! 19. you will choose 20. give!

Exercise 7 1. אָמְרָה 2. אָהֲבָה 3. נָתְנָה 4. כָּתְבָה 5. רָאֲתָה

6. שָׁמָה 7. יֹאמְרוּ 8. יֶאֱהֲבוּ 9. יִתְּנוּ 10. יִשְׁמְרוּ 11. יַעֲשׂוּ

12. יֵשְׁבוּ 13. פָּעַל, imperfect, 2, f, sg, א.מ.ר 14. פָּעַל

15. פָּעַל, imperfect, 3, m, sg, ב.ה.א, pl, m, 3, imperfect

16. פָּעַל, infinitive construct with ל, -,-,-, נ.ת.ן י.שׁ.ב

52

participle, פָּעַל 18. נ.ח.ן, sg, m, active participle, פָּעַל 17.

ז.כ.ר ,sg, f 19. פָּעַל, imperfect, 2, m, pl, נ.ח.ן 20. פָּעַל,

pl, c, 1, imperfect, פָּעַל 21. נ.ח.ן, pl, f, 2, perfect

ש.י.מ. imperat., פָּעַל 23. ב.נ.ה pl, m, 2, perfect, פָּעַל 22.

ע.שׂ.ה, pl, f ב.נ.ה, pl, c, 1, imperfect, פָּעַל 24. ה.

1. she said 2. she loved 3. she gave 4. she wrote 5. she
saw 6. she put 7. they will say 8. they will love 9. they
will give 10. they will guard 11. they will do 12. they
will sit 13. you will say 14. they will love 15. he will
sit 16. to give 17. giving 18. remembering 19. you will
give 20. you gave 21. we will put 22. you built 23. do!
24. we will build

CHAPTER 25

Exercise 2   1. A. גָּדַלְתָּ אֶת הַנַּעַר וְהוּא גָּדַל. B. הָאָבוֹת גִּדְּלוּ...

C. גִּדַּלְתֶּן... D. גִּדַּלְנוּ... E. הָאִישׁ גָּדַל... F. גָּדַלְתְּ...

G. גִּדַּלְתִּי... H. גִּדַּלְתֶּם... I. הַנָּשִׁים גָּדְלוּ... 2. A. הָיוּ בְּהֵמוֹת

רַבּוֹת בַּשָּׂדֶה וַתִּסְפֹּרְנָה הַבָּנוֹת אֹתָן. B. ...וָאֶסְפֹּר... C. ...וַתִּסְפְּרִי

D. ...וַתִּסְפְּרִי... E. ...וַיִּסְפְּרוּ... F. ...גִּדַּלְתְּ...

G. ...וַתִּסְפֹּר... H. ...וַתִּסְפֹּרְנָה... I. ...וַתִּסְפֹּר שָׂרָה...

3. A. הַזְּקֵנִים יִזְכְּרוּ אֶת מַעֲשֵׂיהֶם הַטּוֹבִים וְהֵם יְסַפְּרוּ לָנוּ עֲלֵיהֶם.

B. תִּזְכֹּר אֶת מַעֲשֶׂיךָ הַטּוֹבִים וּתְסַפֵּר לָנוּ עֲלֵיהֶם. C. הִיא תִּזְכֹּר אֶת

מַעֲשֶׂיהָ הַטּוֹבִים וּתְסַפֵּר... D. תִּזְכְּרוּ אֶת מַעֲשֵׂיכֶם הַטּוֹבִים וּתְסַפְּרוּ...

E. הֵנָּה תִּזְכֹּרְנָה אֶת מַעֲשֵׂיהֶן הַטּוֹבִים וּתְסַפֵּרְנָה... F. תִּזְכְּרִי אֶת

מַעֲשַׂיִךְ הַטּוֹבִים וּתְסַפְּרִי... G. תִּזְכֹּרְנָה אֶת מַעֲשֵׂיכֶן הַטּוֹבִים וּתְסַפֵּרְנָה

4. A. ...וַיֹּאמֶר הָאִישׁ לֵאמֹר: "הַשּׁוֹפְטִים מְצַוִּים אֶתְכֶם לַעֲשׂוֹת אֶת

הַמִּצְוֹת." B. ..."הַזְּקֵנוֹת מְצַוּוֹת..." C. ...אֵשֶׁת דָּוִד מְצַוָּה..."

D. ..."אֲנַחְנוּ מְצַוִּים..." 5. A. בִּקַּשְׁתִּי אֶת הָאֱמֶת וְצִוִּיתִי אֶת

הָאֲנָשִׁים לֵאמֹר: "דַּבְּרוּ אֵלַי". B. בִּקַּשְׁתֶּם...וְצִוִּיתֶם..."דַּבְּרוּ אֵלֵינוּ".

Chapter 25

C. הֵנָּה בִּקְשׁוּ...וְצִוּוּ..."דַּבְּרוּ אֵלֵינוּ". D. בִּקַּשְׁתָּ...וְצִוִּיתָ..."דַּבְּרוּ

אֵלַי". E. בִּקַּשְׁנוּ...וְצִוִּינוּ..."דַּבְּרוּ אֵלֵינוּ". F. בִּקַּשְׁתְּ...וְצִוִּיתְ...

דַּבְּרוּ אֵלַי". G. בִּקַּשְׁתֶּן...וְצִוִּיתֶן..."דַּבְּרוּ אֵלֵינוּ". H. הוּא בִּקֵּשׁ...

וְצִוָּה..."דַּבְּרוּ אֵלַי". I. הֵמָּה בִּקְשׁוּ...וְצִוּוּ..."דַּבְּרוּ אֵלֵינוּ".

6. A. דָּוִד סָפַר אֶת כָּל כֵּלָיו וּמִסְפָּרָם לֹא גָּדוֹל. B. סָפַרְנוּ אֶת כָּל

כֵּלֵינוּ... C. שָׂרָה סָפְרָה אֶת כָּל כֵּלֶיהָ... D. הֵנָּה סָפְרוּ אֶת כָּל כְּלֵיהֶן..

E. סְפַרְתֶּם אֶת כָּל כְּלֵיכֶם... F. סָפַרְתִּי אֶת כָּל כֵּלַי... G. סָפַרְתָּ אֶת כָּל

כֵּלֶיךָ... H. הֵמָּה סָפְרוּ אֶת כָּל כְּלֵיהֶם... I. סְפַרְתֶּן אֶת כָּל כְּלֵיכֶן...

1. The mother brought up the lad and he grew up. A. You brought up the lad and he grew up. B. The fathers brought up the lad and he grew up. C. You brought up... D. We brought up ... E. The man brought up... F. You brought up... G. I brought up... H. You brought up... I. The women brought up... 2. There were many animals in the field and the lad counted them. A. There were many animals in the field and the daughters counted them. B. ...and I counted them. C. ...and you counted them. D. ...and you counted them. E. ...and they counted them. F. ...and we counted them. G. ...and you counted them. H. ...and you counted them. I. ...and Sarah counted them. 3. Our father will remember his good deeds and he will recount them to us. A. The old men will remember their good deeds and they will recount them to us. B. You will remember your good deeds and you will recount... C. She will remember her good deeds and she will recount... D. You will remember your good deeds and you will recount... E. They will remember their good deeds and they will recount... F. You will remember your good deeds and you will recount... G. You will remember your good deeds and you will recount... 4. And the man said, saying, "I am commanding you to do the commandments." A. And the man said, saying, "The judges are commanding you to do the commandments." B. ..."The old women are commanding..." C. ..."David's wife is commanding..." D. ..."We are commanding..." 5. She sought the truth and she commanded the people, saying "Speak to me!" A. I sought the truth and I commanded the people, saying "Speak to me!" B. You sought the truth and you commanded the people, saying, "Speak to us!" C. They sought the truth and they commanded the people, saying "Speak to us!" D. You sought the truth and you commanded the people, saying "Speak to me!" E. We sought the truth and we commanded the people, saying "Speak to us!" F. You sought the truth and you commanded the people, saying "Speak to me!" G. You sought the truth and you commanded the people, saying "Speak to us!" H. He sought the truth and he

commanded the people, saying "Speak to me!" I. They sought
the truth and they commanded the people, saying "Speak to
us!" 6. I counted all my vessels, and their number was not
great. A. David counted all his vessels, and their number was
not great. B. We counted all our vessels... C. Sarah counted
all her vessels... D. They counted all their vessels...
E. You counted all your vessels... F. You counted all your
vessels... G. You counted all your vessels... H. They counted
all their vessels... I. You counted all your vessels...

Exercise 3 1. he will come, she came or is coming, to come,
I came, coming, come! 2. to seek, we sought, they/you will
seek, seeking, he sought, we will seek 3. you saw, you will
see, seeing, to see, they saw 4. I will give, give!, you
gave, giving, she gave, to give 5. you/she will command,
they commanded, commanding, to command, command!, you
commanded, I will command 6. speaking, speak!, you spoke, to
speak, speak!, I will speak, you will speak 7. he recounted,
he counted, I counted, I recounted, to count, to recount,
they will recount, they will count, counting, recounting
8. bringing up, you will grow up, you/they will bring up, to
bring up, grow up/big, grow up!, he grew up, he will bring up,
she brought up, we grew up, they grew up

Exercise 4 1. סְפַרְתֶּם, מְסַפְּרִים, תְּסַפְּרוּ, סַפֵּר סְפַרְתֶּם, סַפֵּר תְּסַפְּרוּ,

2. בִּקַּשְׁתָּ, מְבַקֵּשׁ, תְּבַקֵּשׁ, בַּקֵּשׁ בִּקַּשְׁתָּ, בַּקֵּשׁ תְּבַקֵּשׁ, בַּקֵּשׁ 3. צַוֵּה, סָרוּ

מְצַוֶּה, וְצַוָּה, צַוֵּה צַוָּה, צַוֵּה וְצַוָּה 4. גִּדְּלוּ, מְגַדְּלִים, וְגִדְּלוּ, גַּדֵּל

גִּדְּלוּ, גַּדֵּל יְגַדְּלוּ 5. סִפַּרְנוּ, מְסַפְּרִים, נְסַפֵּר, סַפֵּר סִפַּרְנוּ, סַפֵּר נְסַפֵּר;

סָפְרוּ, סוֹפְרִים, יִסְפְּרוּ, סָפוֹר סָפְרוּ, סָפוֹר יִסְפְּרוּ 6. בָּנִיתִי, בּוֹנֶה,

אֶבְנֶה, בָּנֹה בָּנִיתִי, בָּנֹה אֶבְנֶה 7. שָׁבָה, שָׁבָה, שָׁבָה, שׁוֹב שָׁבָה, שׁוֹב

תָּשׁוּב 8. בִּקֵּשׁ, מְבַקֵּשׁ, יְבַקֵּשׁ, בַּקֵּשׁ בִּקֵּשׁ, בַּקֵּשׁ יְבַקֵּשׁ

1. You (recounted, are recounting, will recount, surely
recounted, will surely recount, recount!) to the nations
about the covenant. 2. Upon your return from the wilderness,
you (sought, are seeking, will seek, surely sought, will
surely seek, seek!) your family. 3. He (commanded, is commanding, will command, certainly commanded, will certainly
command) his sons, saying "Give water from the Jordan to the
old men". 4. They (raise, are raising, will raise, surely
raised, will surely raise) many animals in Egypt. 5. We
(related, are relating, will relate, surely related, will
surely relate) to them about the people who (counted, are
counting, will count, really counted, will really count) the
money. 6. I (built, am building, will build, really built,

will really build) a great city in Canaan. 7. She (returned, is returning, will returned, certainly returned, will certainly return) from Egypt to see her mother. 8. Jacob (sought, is seeking, will seek, surely sought, will surely seek) to know the number of his tents.

Exercise 5 1. דִּבַּרְתִּי דְּבָרִים רַבִּים אֶל אַנְשֵׁי הָעִיר. 2. דִּבַּרְתָּ דְּבָרִים רַבִּים אֶל אַנְשֵׁי הָעִיר. 3. תְּדַבֵּר דְּבָרִים רַבִּים אֶל אַנְשֵׁי הָעִיר. 4. עוֹדֶן מְבַקְשׁוֹת אֶת הָאֱמֶת. 5. עוֹדֵנוּ מְבַקְּשִׁים אֶת הָאֱמֶת. 6. עוֹדֵךְ מְבַקֶּשֶׁת אֶת הָאֱמֶת. 7. צִוִּיתִי אֹתָהּ לֵאמֹר: "לְכִי!" 8. הִיא צִוְּתָה אֹתוֹ לֵאמֹר: "לֵךְ!" 9. צִוִּינוּ אֹתָם לֵאמֹר: "לְכוּ!"

Exercise 6 1. כ.ת.ב 2. ק.ו.ם 3. ס.פ.ר 4. ר.א.ה 5. ע.שׂ.ה. 6. א.ה.ב 7. י.ד.ע 8. ב.ו.א 9. צ.ו.ה 10. ג.ד.ל 11. נ.ת.ן 12. ד.ב.ר 13. א.ה.ב 14. ע.שׂ.ה 15. צ.ו.ה 16. ג.ד.ל 17. נ.ת.ן 18. ר.א.ה 19. ד.ב.ר 20. י.ד.ע

פָּעֵל Forms: 3, 9, 12, 15, 16, 19

1. she wrote 2. she arose or is arising 3. recounting 4. see! 5. and she/you did 6. and I loved 7. to know 8. we will come 9. command! 10. grow up 11. you gave 12. you/they will speak 13. to love 14. you did 15. commanding 16. I will bring up 17. give 18. and he saw 19. you spoke 20. you will know

Exercise 7 "The Fisherman and His Wife" There was a fisherman who lived in a very small house with his wife, and they had no money. The man went daily to the sea to fish and he returned in the evening to his house to give food to his wife. And it came to pass one morning that the fisherman went to the sea and fished there. And it was in the evening that the fisherman caught a big fish. And the fish said to the fisherman: "Let me return to my house under the water and I will give you all that you may seek from me." And the fisherman answered the fish, saying: "I must give my wife food. If you give me food instead of you, I will send you to your house under the water." And the fish gave the fisherman wine and bread and fruit, and the man returned to his house. And his wife said to him: "What is this food?" And he recounted to his wife everything that the fish had done for him. And his wife commanded him: "Return to the sea! Command the fish to build a big house for us and to give us money." So the fisherman went, and he came to the sea and he said: "Fish, come! Come up to me!" And the fish came up and said: "What

are you seeking from me?" And he told the fish everything
that his wife had said. The fish said: "Return to your house
and I will do all that you have sought." And the fisherman
returned to his house and behold, everything was as he had
sought from the fish. And his wife said to him: "Return to
the sea! Command the fish to make us like kings and we will
rule over all the land." And the fisherman went, and he came
to the sea and he said: "Fish, come! Come up to me!" And the
fish came up and he said: "What are you seeking from me?"
And he told the fish everything that his wife had said. And
the fish said: "Return to your house and everything will be
as you have sought." And the fisherman returned to his house
and behold, everything was as the fish had said. And the
wife of the fisherman said to him, saying: "Now we are like
kings. Why shouldn't we be gods? Return to the sea! Command
the fish to make us gods and we will rule over both the
earth and the heavens." Now the fisherman answered his wife:
"We are like kings. We must seek only things that belong to
people. I will not go to seek from the fish this thing." The
woman did not pay attention to his words, and she said to
him: "Return to the sea! Do what I have commanded you!" So
the fisherman went, and he came to the sea and he said:
"Fish, come! Come up to me!" And the fish came up and he
said: "What are you still seeking from me?" And he told the
fish everything that his wife had said. Now the fish said:
"You have not sought well! A man is not able to be a god.
Now you will not be gods, and you will also not be kings,
and I will also take both your house and your money from
you. Return to your evil wife! You have sought everything
and now you will not have a thing." And the fisherman
returned to his small house and the fish did not come up to
him from the sea again.

Exercise 8   1. שָׁמַרְתָּ   2. דִּבַּרְתָּ   3. כָּתַבְנוּ   4. בִּקַּשְׁנוּ   5. בָּנִינוּ

6. צִוִּינוּ   7. תִּשְׁמֹר   8. תְּדַבֵּר   9. יִכְתְּבוּ   10. יְבַקְשׁוּ   11. תִּבְנוּ

12. תְּצַוֶּה   13. תִּשְׁמְרִי   14. מְדַבֶּרֶת   15. כּוֹתֶבֶת   16. מְבַקְשִׁים

17. בּוֹנִים   18. תְּצַוֶּה   19. תְּדַבֵּר   20. דִּבְּרָה   21. בִּקֵּשׁ   22. יְבַקֵּשׁ

23. צִוָּה   24. יְצַוֶּה

1. you guarded 2. you spoke 3. we wrote 4. we sought 5. we
built 6. we commanded 7. she will guard 8. she will speak
9. they will write 10. they will seek 11. you will build
12. you will command 13. you will guard 14. speaking
15. writing 16. seeking 17. building 18. you will command
19. you will speak 20. she spoke 21. he sought 22. he will
seek 23. he commanded 24. he will command

CHAPTER 26

Exercise 2 1. A. הַנְּעָרוֹת הִשְׁלִיכוּ אֲבָנִים אֶל תּוֹךְ הַיַּרְדֵּן. B. הִשְׁלַכְתְּ
אֲבָנִים. C. ...הִשְׁלַכְנוּ. D. הוּא הִשְׁלִיךְ... E. ...הִשְׁלַכְתֶּם. F. הִיא
הִשְׁלִיכָה... G. הִשְׁלַכְתִּי... H. הִשְׁלַכְתֶּן... I. הִשְׁלַכְתְּ. 2. A. אֲנִי
מַלְבִּישָׁה אֶת בְּנוֹתַי בַּבֹּקֶר. B. הוּא מַלְבִּישׁ אֶת בְּנוֹתָיו... C. אַתֶּן
מַלְבִּישׁוֹת אֶת בְּנוֹתֵיכֶן... D. אַתְּ מַלְבִּישָׁה אֶת בְּנוֹתַיִךְ... E. הִיא
מַלְבִּישָׁה אֶת בְּנוֹתֶיהָ... F. הֵם מַלְבִּישִׁים אֶת בְּנוֹתֵיהֶם... G. אַתֶּם
מַלְבִּישִׁים אֶת בְּנוֹתֵיכֶם... H. אֲנַחְנוּ מַלְבִּישׁוֹת אֶת בְּנוֹתֵינוּ... I. אַתָּה
מַלְבִּישׁ אֶת בְּנוֹתֶיךָ... 3. A. הָעָם יַמְלִיךְ אֹתוֹ וּמָלַךְ עָלָיו כָּל יְמֵי
חַיָּיו. B. אַנְשֵׁי כְּנַעַן יַמְלִיכוּ...וּמָלַךְ עֲלֵיהֶם... C. תַּמְלִיכוּ...וּמָלַךְ
עֲלֵיכֶם. D. אַמְלִיךְ...וּמָלַךְ עָלַי... E. תַּמְלַכְנָה...וּמָלַךְ עֲלֵיכֶן...
F. תַּמְלִיכִי...וּמָלַךְ עָלַיִךְ. G. תַּמְלִיךְ...וּמָלַךְ עָלֶיהָ... H. הֵנָּה
יַמְלִיכוּ...וּמָלַךְ עֲלֵיהֶם... I. הִיא תַּמְלִיךְ...וּמָלַךְ עָלֶיהָ...
4. A. הָאָב גִּדֵּל אֶת הַבָּנִים וְכַאֲשֶׁר הַבָּנִים גָּדְלוּ הֵם הִגְדִּילוּ אֶת בֵּית
מִשְׁפַּחְתָּם. B. ...אָחִי וְכַאֲשֶׁר גָּדַלְתִּי הִגְדַּלְתִּי אֶת בֵּית מִשְׁפַּחְתִּי.
C. ...אֶתְכֶן וְכַאֲשֶׁר גְּדַלְתֶּן הִגְדַּלְתֶּן אֶת בֵּית מִשְׁפַּחְתְּכֶן. D. ...אֹתָךְ
וְכַאֲשֶׁר גָּדַלְתְּ הִגְדַּלְתְּ אֶת בֵּית מִשְׁפַּחְתֵּךְ. E. ...אֹתָנוּ וְכַאֲשֶׁר גָּדַלְנוּ
הִגְדַּלְנוּ אֶת בֵּית מִשְׁפַּחְתֵּנוּ. F. ...אֶת הַבָּנוֹת וְכַאֲשֶׁר הַבָּנוֹת גָּדְלוּ הֵנָּה
הִגְדִּילוּ אֶת בֵּית מִשְׁפַּחְתָּן. G. ...אֶתְכֶם וְכַאֲשֶׁר גְּדַלְתֶּם הִגְדַּלְתֶּם אֶת בֵּית
מִשְׁפַּחְתְּכֶם. H. ...אֹתָהּ וְכַאֲשֶׁר גָּדְלָה הִגְדִּילָה אֶת בֵּית מִשְׁפַּחְתָּהּ. I. ...אֶת
הַנַּעֲרָה וְכַאֲשֶׁר הַנַּעֲרָה גָּדְלָה הִיא הִגְדִּילָה אֶת בֵּית מִשְׁפַּחְתָּהּ. 5. A. וַיַּגֵּד
הָאִישׁ לָהֶם לֵאמֹר: "אֶת מַעֲשֵׂי אֲבוֹתֵיכֶם הֵמָּה יַזְכִּירוּ לָכֶם וְזִכֹר תִּזְכְּרוּ
אֹתָם." B. ...בַּזְכִּיר לָהֶם. C. ...הֵנָּה תַּזְכֵּרְנָה לָהֶם. D. ...הִיא
תַּזְכִּיר... E. ...הוּא יַזְכִּיר... 6. A. הִצַּלְתִּי אֶת אַנְשֵׁי הָעִיר הַהִיא.
B. הֵנָּה הִצִּילוּ... C. ...הִצַּלְתְּ. D. הִיא הִצִּילָה... E. ...הִצַּלְנוּ.

F. ‏...הִצַּלְתֶּן‏ G. ‏הֵמָּה הִצִּילוּ...‏ H. ‏הִצַּלְתְּ...‏ I. ‏הִצַּלְתֶּם...‏

1. The sons threw stones into the Jordan. A. The maidens
threw stones into the Jordan. B. You threw... C. We threw..
D. He threw... E. You threw... F. She threw... G. I threw..
H. You threw... I. You threw... 2. These women are dressing
their daughters in the morning. A. I am dressing my
daughters in the morning. B. He is dressing his daughters..
C. You are dressing your daughters... D. You are dressing
your daughters... E. She is dressing her daughters...
F. They are dressing their daughters... G. You are dressing
your daughters... H. We are dressing our daughters...
I. You are dressing your daughters... 3. We will make him
king and he will rule over us all the days of his life.
A. The nation will make him king and he will rule over it
all the days of his life. B. The people of Canaan will make
him king and he will rule over them... C. You will make him
king and he will rule over you... D. I will make him king
and he will rule over me... E. You will make him king and
he will rule over me... F. You will make him king and he
will rule over you... G. You will make him king and he will
rule over you... H. They will make him king and he will
rule over them... I. She will make him king and he will
rule over her... 4. The father brought up the lad and when
the lad grew up, he made the house of his family great.
A. The father brought up the sons and when the sons grew up
they made the house of their family great. B...me up, and
when I grew up, I made the house of my family great.
C...you up, and when you grew up you made the house of your
family great. D...you up and when you grew up, you made the
house of your family great. E...us up and when we grew up,
we made the house of our family great. F...the daughters
and when the daughters grew up, they made the house of
their family great. G...you up and when you grew up, you
made the house of your family great. H...you up, and when
you grew up, you made the house of your family great.
I...the maiden up, and when the maiden grew up she made the
house of her family great. 5. And the man told them,
saying: "I will mention to you the deeds of your fathers
and you will surely remember them." A. And the man told
them, saying: "They will mention to you the deeds of your
fathers and you will surely remember them." B. ..."We will
mention..." C. ..."They will mention..." D. ..."She will
mention..." E. ..."He will mention..." 6. Jacob rescued
the people of that city. A. I rescued the people of that
city. B. They rescued... C. You rescued... D. She rescued..
E. We rescued... F. You rescued... G. They rescued...
H. You rescued... I. You rescued...

Exercise 3 ‎1. הִשְׁלַכְתָּ, מַשְׁלִיכָה, תַּשְׁלִיכִי, הַשְׁלֵהַ הִשְׁלַכְתָּ, תַּשְׁלֶה

‎2. הִצַּלְתֶּם, מַצִּילִים, תַּצִּילוּ, הַצֵּל הִצַּלְתֶּם, הַצֵּל תַּשְׁלִיכִי, הַשְׁלִיכִי

‎3. הִמְלִיךְ, מַמְלִיךְ, יַמְלִיךְ, הַמְלֵךְ הִמְלִיךְ, הַמְלֵךְ יַמְלִיךְ תַּצִּילוּ, הַצִּילוּ

‎4. הִזְכַּרְתָּ, מַזְכִּיר, תַּזְכִּיר, הַזְכֵּר הִזְכַּרְתָּ, הַזְכֵּר תַּזְכִּיר, הַזְכֵּר; זָכְרוּ,

זוֹכְרִים, יִזְכְּרוּ, זָכוֹר זָכְרוּ, זָכוֹר יִזְכְּרוּ ‎5. בִּקַּשְׁתָּ, מְבַקְשׁוֹת,

תְּבַקֵּשְׁנָה, בַּקֵּשׁ בִּקַּשְׁתָּ, בַּקֵּשׁ תְּבַקֵּשְׁנָה, בַּקֵּשְׁנָה ‎6. נָתְנוּ, נוֹתְנִים, יִתְּנוּ,

נָתוֹן נָתְנוּ, נָתוֹן יִתְּנוּ ‎7. קַמְנוּ, קָמִים, נָקוּם, קוֹם קַמְנוּ, קוֹם
נָקוּם

1. You (threw, are throwing, will throw, really threw, will really throw, throw!) your shoes upon the ground. 2. You (saved, are saving, will save, certainly saved, will certainly save, save!) the women from the evil men. 3. The nation (crowned, is crowning, will crown, surely crowned, will surely crown) David as king over Israel. 4. You (reminded, are reminding, will remind, really reminded, will really remind, remind!) the old ones of Bethlehem, and they (remembered, are remembering, will remember, surely remembered, will surely remember) the people there. 5. You (sought, are seeking, will seek, certainly sought, will certainly seek, seek!) to save the maiden from the midst of the sea. 6. They (gave, are giving, will give, surely gave, will surely give) new clothes to the women to dress their sons. 7. We (arose, are arising, will arise, surely arose, will surely arise) to tell the truth to all the city.

Exercise 4   1. And the lad ran to the city and he told the people all that he had seen. 2. And she/you saw his good works and made him king. 3. And the mother gave her son water to drink and dressed him in new garments. 4. And he heard the voice of a woman, and he saw her in the water, and he turned aside from the road and saved her, and took her to the house of her father.

Shortened Verbs ‎1. וַיָּרָץ, וַיַּגֵּד ‎2. וַתֵּרֶא, וַתַּמְלֵךְ ‎3. וַתַּלְבֵּשׁ
‎4. וַיַּרְא, וַיָּסַר, וַיַּצֵּל

Exercise 5 ‎1. ג.ד.ל - פָּעַל ‎2. נ.צ.ל - הִפְעִיל ‎3. שׁ.י.ר - פָּעַל
‎4. ב.נ.ה - פָּעַל ‎5. ד.ב.ר - פִּעֵל ‎6. ג.ד.ל - הִפְעִיל ‎7. שׁ.ל.ך -
הִפְעִיל ‎8. ז.כ.ר - הִפְעִיל ‎9. ב.נ.ה - פָּעַל ‎10. ג.ד.ל - פָּעַל

11. נ.צ.ל - הִפְעִיל   12. ז.כ.ר - הִפְעִיל   13. שׁ.י.ר - פָּעַל

14. ד.ב.ר - פָּעַל   15. שׁ.ל.ךְ - הִפְעִיל

1. I will grow up 2. saving 3. to sing 4. he will build
5. we spoke 6. make great! 7. to throw 8. I reminded
9. building 10. making great 11. we rescued 12. reminding
13. she sang/is singing 14. I will speak 15. they threw

Exercise 6 1. Next week, they will make me king because...
2. Year by year I will tell my family... 3. Daily I make my
name great because... 4. My brothers threw stones at me
because... 5. You rescued the lad who...

Exercise 7 הָיָה, בִּקֵּשׁ, בָּא, הָיָה, לָבַשׁ, עָשׂוֹת, יוּכְלוּ, רְאוֹת, תֵּן,

אֶעֱשֶׂה, לָדַעַת, עָשָׂה, אֶלְבַּשׁ, אַגְדִּיל, לָקַח, שָׁלַח, רְאוֹת, הָיָה, רוֹאֶה, יָדַע

יוּכְלוּ, רְאוֹת, שָׁב, הִגִּיד, צִוָּה, אֶלְבַּשׁ, בּוֹא, רְאוֹת, יָדַע, יוּכְלוּ,

רְאוֹת, בָּא, רָאָה, אָמַר, הָיְתָה, הִגִּידָה, בָּאָה, רָאָה, צִוָּה, בִּקֵּשׁ, הָלַךְ

There was an evil man who sought much money, and his name
was Aaron. One day, Aaron came to a great city. In that city
there was a king who always wore new clothes. So Aaron went
to the king's house and said: "I can make clothes for you
that are not like any others in all your land. Only wise men
can see these clothes. Give me money, and I will make them
for you." The king said to himself: "I will be a very great
king. I will be able to know who is wise and who is not wise."
And the king answered and said: "Behold, the money, and now
make for me these clothes, and I will wear them and make my
name great in the land." Aaron took the king's money and went
to make the clothes for the king. After these things, the
king sent his lad to Aaron to see the clothes he was
making. When the lad came to Aaron's house, he saw that
there were no clothes there. The lad said to himself: "I
don't see the clothes." The lad knew that only wise men
could see the clothes. So the lad said to Aaron: "I see the
new clothes. There are none like them in all the land." The
lad returned to his king, and told him that he had seen the
king's new clothes. The king commanded all his people,
saying: "Next week I will put on my new clothes. You must
come to see me." All the people knew that only wise men
could see these clothes. On that week, the people came to
the house of the king. And behold, all the people saw that
there were no clothes on the king. Every man said to himself
"I am not wise, because I don't see the king's clothes."
Among all the people there was a young woman who had come
with her father. She said: "See! The king doesn't have
clothes!" All the people knew that the young woman had told

the truth. The king saw that he was naked, and ran inside
his house. He commanded his lads to seek Aaron and to kill
him. But Aaron was not in the city. He had gone, and all the
king's money with him.

Exercise 8 1. פָּתַחְתָּ 2. הִשְׁלַכְתָּ 3. הִצַּלְתָּ 4. זוֹכְרוֹת

5. מַזְכִּירוֹת 6. מַגִּידוֹת 7. תִּמְלֹךְ 8. תַּמְלִיךְ 9. תַּגִּיד

1. you opened 2. you threw 3. you rescued 4. remembering
5. reminding 6. telling 7. she will rule 8. she will crown
9. she will tell

CHAPTER 27

Exercise 2 1. A. בָּעֵת הַהִיא הוּא הֵקִים בַּיִת חָדָשׁ בָּעִיר. B. בָּעֵת

הַהִיא הֵנָּה הֵקִימוּ... C. ...הֲקִימוֹת/הֲקַמְתְּ... D. ...הֲקִימוֹנוּ/הֲקַמְנוּ

... E. ...הִיא הֵקִימָה... F. ...הֲקִימוֹת/הֲקַמְתְּ... G. ...הֲקִימוֹתִי

/הֲקַמְתִּי... H. ...הֲקִימוֹתֶן... I. ...הֵמָּה הֵקִימוּ... 2. A. הַשַּׂר

צִוָּה אֶת אֲנָשָׁיו לְהָשִׁיב אֶת אַנְשֵׁי בֵּית לֶחֶם. B. ...לְהַגְדִּיל...

C. ...לְהָבִיא... D. ...לְהַזְכִּיר/לִזְכֹּר... E. ...לְהָסִיר...

3. A. בָּעֵת הַהִיא אָסִיר אֶת בְּגָדָיו וְאַלְבִּישׁ אֹתוֹ בִּגְדֵי שַׂר. B. ...הוּא

יָסִיר...וְיַלְבִּישׁ... C. ...תָּסִירָנָה...וְתַלְבֵּשְׁנָה... D. ...תָּסִיר...

וְתַלְבִּישׁ... E. ...הִיא תָּסִיר...וְתַלְבִּישׁ... F. ...הֵנָּה תָּסִירְנָה...

וְתַלְבֵּשְׁנָה... G. ...נָסִיר...וְנַלְבִּישׁ... H. ...תָּסִירוּ...וְתַלְבִּישׁוּ...

I. ...תָּסִירִי...וְתַלְבִּישִׁי... 4. A. אַתְּ מְכִינָה אֶת הָאֹכֶל לַשַּׂר. B. אַתֶּם

מְכִינִים... C. הֵנָּה מְכִינוֹת... D. אַתָּה מֵכִין... E. אָנֹכִי מֵכִין...

F. אַתֶּן מְכִינוֹת... G. הוּא מֵכִין... H. הִיא מְכִינָה... 5. A. הֵמָּה

יָשׁוּבוּ מֵהֶהָרִים וְיָבִיאוּ לָנוּ כֶּסֶף וְזָהָב. B. הַנָּשִׁים תָּשֹׁבְנָה...וְתָבֵאנָה...

C. אָשׁוּב...וְאָבִיא... D. הִיא תָּשׁוּב...וְתָבִיא... E. תָּשׁוּב...וְתָבִיא...

F. תָּשֹׁבְנָה...וְתָבֵאנָה... G. נָשׁוּב...וְנָבִיא... H. תָּשׁוּבִי...וְתָבִיאִי...

I. תָּשׁוּבוּ...וְתָבִיאוּ... 6. A. הֵם שָׁבוּ מִמִּצְרַיִם וְהֵשִׁיבוּ אֶת הַנַּעַר

לְמִשְׁפַּחְתּוֹ ... B. שַׁבְתֶּן...וַהֲשִׁיבוֹתֶן ... C. שַׁבְנוּ...וְהֵשַׁבְנוּ ... D. הוּא

שָׁב...וְהֵשִׁיב ... E. הֵנָּה שָׁבוּ...וְהֵשִׁיבוּ ... F. שַׁבְתִּי...וַהֲשִׁיבוֹתִי...

G. הִיא שָׁבָה...וְהֵשִׁיבָה ... H. שַׁבְתֶּם...וַהֲשִׁיבוֹתֶם ... I. שָׁבְתָּ...

וְהֵשַׁבְתָּ ... 7. A. אֵינְכֶם מְבִינִים אֶת אֲשֶׁר הֵנָּה סְפָרוֹ לָכֶם. B. אֵינֶנּוּ

מֵבִין...לוֹ. C. אֵינְךָ מֵבִין...לָהּ. D. אֵינָן מְבִינוֹת...לָהֶן.

E. אֵינֵךְ מְבִינָה...לָךְ. F. אֵינְכֶן מְבִינוֹת...לָכֶן. G. אֵינֶנָּה מְבִינָה

...לָהּ. H. אֵינֶנּוּ מְבִינִים...לָנוּ. I. אֵינָם מְבִינִים...לָהֶם.

1. At that time, you established a new house in the city.
A. At that time, he established a new house in the city.
B. ...they established... C. ...you established... D. ...we
established... E. ...she established... F. ...you established... G. ...I established... H. ...you established...
I. ...they established... 2. The officer commanded his men
to rescue the people of Bethlehem. A. The officer commanded
his men to bring back the people of Bethlehem. B. ...to make
great... C. ...to bring... D. ...to mention/to remember...
E. ...to remove... 3. At that time, they will remove his
clothes and they will dress him in clothes of an officer.
A.At that time, I will remove his clothes and I will dress
him in clothes of an officer. B...he will remove...and he
will dress...C....you will remove...and you will dress...
D. ...you will remove...and you will dress... E. ...she will
remove...and she will dress... F. ...they will remove...and
they will dress... G. ...we will remove...and we will dress
... H. ...you will remove...and you will dress... I. ...you
will remove...and you will dress... 4. We are preparing the
food for the chief. A. You are preparing the food for the
chief. B. You are preparing... C. They are preparing...
D. You are preparing... E. I am preparing... F. You are preparing... G. He is preparing... H. She is preparing... 5. He
will return from the mountains and will bring us silver and
gold. A. They will return from the mountains and will bring
us silver and gold. B. The women will return...and will
bring... C. I will return...and will bring... D. She will
return...and will bring... E. You will return...and will
bring... F. You will return...and will bring... G. We will
return...and will bring... H. You will return...and will
bring... I. You will return...and will bring... 6. You
returned from Egypt and brought the lad back to his family.
A. They returned from Egypt and brought the lad back to his
family. B. You returned...and brought the lad back... C. We
returned...and brought the lad back... D. He returned...and
brought the lad back... E. They returned...and brought the
lad back... F. I returned...and brought the lad back...

G. She returned...and brought the lad back... H. You returned...and brought the lad back... I. You returned...and
brought the lad back... 7. I do not understand what they
related to me. A. You do not understand what they related to
you. B. He does not understand...to him. C. You do not
understand...to you. D. They do not understand...to them.
E. You do not understand...to you. F. You do not understand
...to you. G. She does not understand...to her. H. We do not
understand...to us. I. They do not understand...to them.

Exercise 3 ‏1. סָרְתֶּם, סָרִים, תָּסוּרוּ, סוֹר סַרְתֶּם, סוֹר תָּסוּרוּ, סוּרוּ;‎

‏הֲסִירוֹתֶם, מְסִירִים, תָּסִירוּ, הָסֵר הֲסִירוֹתֶם, הָסֵר תָּסִירוּ, הָסִירוּ‎

‏2. שַׁבְתֶּן, שָׁבוֹת, תָּשֹׁבְנָה, שׁוֹב שַׁבְתֶּן, שׁוֹב תָּשֹׁבְנָה, שֹׁבְנָה; הֲשִׁיבוֹתֶן,‎

‏מְשִׁיבוֹת, תָּשֵׁבְנָה, הָשֵׁב הֲשִׁיבוֹתֶן, הָשֵׁב תָּשֵׁבְנָה, 3. בָּאת, בָּאָה,‎

‏תָּבוֹאִי, בּוֹא בָּאת, בּוֹא תָּבוֹאִי, בּוֹאִי; הֲבֵאת, מְבִיאָה, תָּבִיאִי, הָבֵא‎

‏הֲבֵאת, הָבֵא תָּבִיאִי, הָבִיאִי 4. קָמוּ, קָמוּ, יָקוּמוּ, קוֹם קָמוּ, קוֹם‎

‏יָקוּמוּ; הֲקִימוּ, מְקִימִים, יָקִימוּ, הָקֵם הֲקִימוּ, הָקֵם יָקִימוּ 5. הִגִּיד,‎

‏מַגִּיד, יַגִּיד, הַגֵּד הִגִּיד, הַגֵּד יַגִּיד 6. בִּקְשָׁה, מְבַקֶּשֶׁת, תְּבַקֵּשׁ, בַּקֵּשׁ‎

‏בִּקְשָׁה, בַּקֵּשׁ תְּבַקֵּשׁ 7. הֲבִינוֹנוּ, מְבִינִים, נָבִין, הָבֵן הֲבִינוֹנוּ, הָבֵן‎

‏נָבִין‎

1. You (turned aside, are turning aside, will turn aside,
surely turned aside, will surely turn aside, turn aside!) to
see the top of the mountain and (removed, are removing, will
remove, surely removed, will surely remove) the stones from
the road. 2. You (returned, are returning, will return,
surely returned, will surely return, return!) to the land of
your fathers and (brought back, are bringing back, will
bring back, surely brought back, will surely bring back,
bring back!) with you the gold and the silver. 3. You (came,
are coming, will come, surely came, will surely come, come!)
to see my father and (brought, are bringing, will bring,
surely brought, will surely bring, bring!) him fruit.
4. They (arose, are arising, will arise, surely arose, will
surely arise) and (set up, are setting up, will set up,
surely set up, will surely set up) the gate of their city.
5. The officer (told, is telling, will tell, surely told,
will surely tell) his men what they must do. 6. She (sought
is seeking, will seek, surely sought, will surely seek) to
know the truth. 7. We (understood, are understanding, will
understand, surely understood, will surely understand) the
words of the judge.

Exercise 4   1. And the wise man came at that time from the top of the mountain and he brought his son with him. 2. And the officer returned from Canaan, and he brought the gold back with him, and he told us all that he had heard there. 3. And the evil men sought to take away the officer, and David rescued him.   4. And the man ate and drank at evening-time, and the woman removed the food. 5. And the man went to Jerusalem, and he built his house there, and he made his family great.

Shortened Verbs   1. וַיָּבֹא   2. וַיֵּשֶׁב, וַיֵּשֶׁב, וַיַּגֵּד   3. וַיֵּצֵא

4. וַיֵּשְׁתְּ, וַתָּסַר   5. וַיִּבֶן, וַיִּגְדַּל

Exercise 5   1. ב.ח.ר - פָּעַל   2. ג.נ.ב - פָּעַל   3. ז.כ.ר - פָּעַל

4. י.ד.ע - פָּעַל   5. א.כ.ל - פָּעַל   6. י.כ.ל - פָּעַל   7. י.שׁ.ב -

פָּעַל   8. שׁ.ו.ב - פָּעַל   9. שׁ.ו.ב - הִפְעִיל   10. שׁ.ו.ב - הִפְעִיל

11. ב.ו.א - פָּעַל   12. ב.ו.א - פָּעַל   13. ב.ו.א - הִפְעִיל

14. ב.ו.א - הִפְעִיל   15. ק.ו.ם - הִפְעִיל   16. ק.ו.ם - פָּעַל

17. ר.א.ה - פָּעַל   18. ר.א.ה - פָּעַל   19. כ.ו.ן - הִפְעִיל

20. כ.ו.ן - הִפְעִיל

1. I chose 2. you/she will steal 3. remembering 4. to know 5. eating 6. I will be able 7. I sat 8. I returned 9. he will bring back 10. you/they will bring back 11. they came 12. come 13. they will bring 14. bringing 15. to set up 16. they arose 17. they saw 18. see! 19. preparing 20. I will prepare

Exercise 6   There was a man who lived in Moab, and his name was Simon. He was very strong, but not very wise. Now Simon sought to make his name great. And he heard that the men of Babel were building a tower, with its top in the heavens. And Simon said to himself: "I will go to Babel and I will build the tower. I will be able to command the men to do everything, because I am very strong." And Simon went, and he came to Babel, and he saw the men who were building the tower. And Simon said to them: "I am Simon! I have come to be chief over you. I can set up great stones for the tower, because I am very strong." And one man answered: "Buenos Dias!" And Simon said: "What?" And another man answered: "Aloha!" And Simon said: "What?!" And another man said: "I can't understand a word you're saying. Why don't you just speak in English?" And Simon said: "What are you saying? I don't understand you." And one old man heard Simon's words and he ran to him and said: "You are speaking like me! There are no people in this place who speak like us." And the old man related to Simon, saying: "When I arose in the morning, and heard the words of my wife, I did not understand what she said. I sought to speak with my sons, and they did not understand my words. I commanded them to build the tower with the men of the city, and they did not obey me. I went to relate the evil deeds of my sons to the men of my city, and none of them understood me. All of the men of this city do not understand one another." And Simon said: "I came to be chief over the men who are building the tower. But I will not be able to command them if they will they will not understand what I say to them. I will go to another city to make my name great there." And Simon said: "Shalom!" and he left. And the old man answered: "Shalom!" And another man answered: "Adios!" And another man answered: "Bon voyage!" And another man answered: "Ciao!" And another man answered: "See you later!"

Exercise 7   1. שָׁכַחְתָּ   2. זָכַרְתָּ   3. הִזְכַּרְתָּ   4. הִצַּלְתָּ   5. בָּאתֶם

6. הֲבֵאתֶם   7. הֲכִינוֹתֶם   8. הֲשִׁיבוֹנוּ/הֵשַׁבְנוּ   9. רָאִינוּ   10. נִשְׁתֶּה

11. נִסְפֹּר   12. נְסַפֵּר   13. אֲדַבֵּר   14. אֲצַוֶּה   15. אַעֲלֶה   16. אַגְדִּיל

17. מַשְׁלִיכָה   18. מְסִירָה   19. מֵקִים   20. קָם   21. קוּם   22. הָקֵם

23. הָקִימִי   24. הָקֵמְנָה

1. you forgot 2. you remembered 3. you reminded 4. you saved 5. you came 6. you brought 7. you prepared 8. we brought back 9. we saw 10. we will drink 11. we will count 12. we will recount 13. I will speak 14. I will command 15. I will bring up 16. I will make great 17. throwing 18. removing 19. establishing 20. arising 21. arise! 22. set up! 23. set up! 24. set up!

CHAPTER 28

1. Exercise 2   A. כַּאֲשֶׁר נִלְחַמְתֶּם בַּמִּלְחָמָה, נִשְׁפַּךְ דָּם רַב.   B. כַּאֲשֶׁר

נִלְחַמְתִּי...   C. כַּאֲשֶׁר הֵמָּה נִלְחֲמוּ...   D. כַּאֲשֶׁר נִלְחַמְתֶּן...   E. כַּאֲשֶׁר

הוּא נִלְחַם...   F. כַּאֲשֶׁר נִלְחַמְתְּ...   G. כַּאֲשֶׁר הִיא נִלְחֲמָה...   H. כַּאֲשֶׁר

נִלְחַמְתָּ...   I. כַּאֲשֶׁר הֵנָּה נִלְחֲמוּ...   2. A. תִּזְכְּרוּ כִּי הֱיִיתֶם אֲנָשִׁים

גִּבּוֹרִים וְהָיָה לָכֶם חֲרָבוֹת רַבּוֹת.   B. הֵמָּה יִזְכְּרוּ כִּי הָיָה הָיוּ אֲנָשִׁים

גִּבּוֹרִים וְהָיוּ לָהֶם... C. הוּא יִזָּכֵר כִּי הוּא הָיָה אִישׁ גִּבּוֹר וְהָיוּ לוֹ
... D. נִזָּכֵר כִּי הָיִינוּ אֲנָשִׁים גִּבּוֹרִים וְהָיוּ לָנוּ... E. תִּזָּכֵר כִּי
הָיִיתָ אִישׁ גִּבּוֹר וְהָיוּ לְךָ... F. אֶזָּכֵר כִּי הָיִיתִי אִישׁ גִּבּוֹר וְהָיוּ לִי
... 3. A. אִישׁ מִמִּשְׁפַּחְתֵּנוּ יִבָּחֵר כִּי הוּא מַלְאַךְ הַמֶּלֶךְ. B. אִישׁ
מִמִּשְׁפַּחְתֵּנוּ יִלָּקַח... C. ...יִשָּׁכַח... D. ...יִזָּכֵר... 4. A. אֵינֶנִּי
נִשְׁכָּח כִּי נָתַתִּי אֵילִים רַבִּים לְמַלְכִּי כְּמִנְחָה. B. אֵינֶנּוּ נִשְׁכָּח כִּי הוּא
נָתַן...לְמַלְכּוֹ... C. אֵינְךָ נִשְׁכַּח כִּי נָתַתָּ...לְמַלְכֶּךָ... D. אֵינְכֶם
נִשְׁכָּחִים כִּי נְתַתֶּם...לְמַלְכְּכֶם... E. אֵינָן נִשְׁכָּחוֹת כִּי נָתְנוּ...לְמַלְכָּן...
F. אֵינֶנּוּ נִשְׁכָּחִים כִּי נָתַנּוּ...לְמַלְכֵּנוּ... G. אֵינְכֶן נִשְׁכָּחוֹת כִּי נְתַתֶּן
...לְמַלְכְּכֶן... H. ...אֵינְךָ נִשְׁכָּח כִּי נָתַתְּ...לְמַלְכֵּךְ... I. אֵינֶנָּה נִשְׁכַּחַת
כִּי נָתְנָה...לְמַלְכָּהּ... 5. A. אִישׁ גִּבּוֹר בָּא אֶל הַשַּׂר לְהִשָּׁמֵר... B. ...
לְהִשָּׁמַע... C. ...לְהִשָּׁפֵט... D. ...לְהִזָּכֵר... E. ...לְהִלָּחֵם.
6. A. נִשְׁלַחְנוּ לְהָבִיא חֲרָבוֹת לָאֲנָשִׁים הַנִּלְחָמִים בַּמִּלְחָמָה. B. נִשְׁלַחְתֶּן...
C. נִשְׁלַחְתָּ... D. הַשַּׂר נִשְׁלַח... E. נָשִׁים נִשְׁלְחוּ... F. נִשְׁלַחְתִּי...
G. נִשְׁלַחְתָּ... H. נִשְׁלַחְתֶּם... I. שָׂרָה נִשְׁלְחָה... 7. A. רְאִיתֶם אֶת
הַדָּם אֲשֶׁר נִשְׁפַּךְ עַל הָאָרֶץ וְרָצִיתֶם מֵהַמָּקוֹם הַהוּא. B. רָאִינוּ...וְרָצִינוּ...
C. הֵנָּה רָאוּ...וְרָצוּ... D. רָאִיתִי...וְרָצִיתִי... E. רָאִיתָ...וְרָצִתָ...
F. רָאִית...וְרָצִת... G. הֵמָּה רָאוּ...וְרָצוּ... H. רְאִיתֶן...וְרָצִתֶן...
I. הִיא רָאֲתָה...וְרָצְתָה...

1. When we fought in the battle, much blood was shed.
A. When you fought in the battle, much blood was shed.
B. When I fought... C. When they fought... D. When you
fought... E. When he fought... F. When you fought... G. When
she fought... H. When you fought... I. When they fought...
2. David will be remembered because he was a mighty man, and
he had many swords. A. You will be remembered because you
were mighty men, and you had many swords. B. They will be
remembered because they were mighty men, and they had...
C. He will be remembered because he was a mighty man, and he
had... D. We will be remembered because we were mighty men,
and we had... E. You will be remembered because you were a
mighty man, and you had... I will be remembered because I

was a mighty man, and I had... 3. A man from our family will
be sent because he is the king's messenger. A. A man from
our family will be chosen because he is the king's messenger
B. A man from our family will be taken... C. ...will be
forgotten... D. ...will be remembered... 4. They are not
being forgotten because they gave many rams to their king as
a gift. A. I am not being forgotten because I gave many rams
to my king as a gift. B. He is not being forgotten because
he gave...to his king... C. You are not being forgotten
because you gave...to your king... D. You are not being
forgotten because you gave... to your king... E. They are
not being forgotten because they gave...to their king...
F. We are not being forgotten because we gave...to our king
... G. You are not being forgotten because you gave...to
your king... H. You are not being forgotten because you gave
...to your king... I. She is not being forgotten because she
gave...to her king... 5. A mighty man came to the chief to
be chosen. A. A mighty man came to the chief to be guarded.
B. ...to be heard. C. ...to be judged. D. ...to be remembered. E. ...to do battle. 6. The lads were sent to bring
swords to the men who were fighting in the battle. A. We
were sent to bring swords to the men who were fighting in
the battle. B. You were sent... C. You were sent... D. The
captain was sent... E. Women were sent... F. I was sent...
G. You were sent... H. You were sent... I. Sarah was sent...
7. The messenger from Bethlehem saw the blood that was spilt
on the land and ran from that place. A. You saw the blood
that was spilt on the land and ran from that place. B. We
saw...and ran... C. They saw...and ran... D. I saw...and ran
... E. You saw...and ran... F. You saw...and ran... G. They
saw...and ran... H. You saw...and ran... I. She saw...and
ran...

Exercise 3 1. הָאַיִל יֻלַּקח מֵהַשָּׂדֶה. 2. דִּבְרֵי הַשַּׂר יִשָּׁמְעוּ. 3. אִשָּׁתוֹ

נִבְחָרֶת. 4. הַחַיִל יִזָּכֵר. 5. מַלְאָךְ נִשְׁלַח. 6. דַּם חֵיל מִצְרַיִם נִשְׁפַּךְ.

1. A man will take the ram from the field. The ram will be
taken from the field. 2. We will hear the words of the
officer because he is a mighty man of valor. The words of
the officer will be heard. 3. The man is choosing his wife
from among the women of Egypt. The wife is chosen. 4. They
will remember the great army that was in the city. The army
will be remembered. 5. You sent a messenger to recount to
the king the number of the armies of Moab. A messenger was
sent. 6. He shed the blood of the army of Egypt in the
battle. The blood of the army of Egypt was shed.

Exercise 4 1. הֵמָּה כָּתְבוּ אֶת הַמִּצְוֹת. 2. אֲנַחְנוּ פוֹתְחִים אֶת שַׁעֲרֵי

הָעִיר כָּל בֹּקֶר. 3. הִיא תְּשַׁבַּח אֶת מַעֲשֶׂיהָ הַטּוֹבִים. 4. תִּשְׁפְּטוּ אֶת הַנָּשִׁים

68

‏5. שָׁפַכְתִּי אֶת הַמַּיִם עַל הָאֲדָמָה.   6. הוּא יִכְתֹּב סְפָרִים עַל חֵיל דָּוִד.

1. The commandments were written. They wrote the commandments. 2. The gates of the city are opened every morning. We open the gates of the city every morning. 3. Your good deeds will be forgotten. She will forget your good deeds. 4. At that time, the women will be judged. You will judge the women. 5. The water in the vessel was poured out on the ground. I poured out the water on the ground. 6. Books will be written about David's army. He will write books about David's army.

‏Exercise 5   1. סָפַר   2. סִפֵּר   3. הִזְכִּיר   4. נִזְכַּר   5. נִסְפֹּר

‏6. נְסַפֵּר   7. נַזְכִּיר   8. נִזָּכֵר   9. סָפַרְתָּ   10. סִפַּרְתָּ   11. הִזְכַּרְתָּ

‏12. נִזְכַּרְתָּ   13. סָפְרָה   14. סִפְּרָה   15. הִזְכִּירָה   16. נִזְכְּרָה

‏17. סוֹפְרִים   18. מְסַפְּרִים   19. מַזְכִּירִים   20. נִזְכָּרִים   21. סְפֹר

‏22. סַפֵּר   23. הַזְכֵּר

1. he counted 2. he recounted 3. he reminded 4. he was remembered 5. we will count 6. we will recount 7. we will remind 8. we will be remembered 9. you counted 10. you recounted 11. you reminded 12. you were remembered 13. she counted 14. she recounted 15. she reminded 16. she was remembered 17. counting 18. recounting 19. reminding 20. being remembered 21. count! 22. recount! 23. remind!

‏Exercise 6   1a. בֹּעַז יִזְכֹּר אִשָּׁה.   1b. בֹּעַז יִזְכֹּר אֶת אִמּוֹ.   1c. בֹּעַז

‏זָכַר אֶת אֵם רוּת.   1d. אֵם רוּת נִזְכְּרָה.   1e. אֲבִי רוּת יִזָּכֵר כְּאִישׁ

‏גִּבּוֹר.   1f. נִזְכַּר בָּאָרֶץ יְהוּדָה פַּעַם קָדוֹשׁ.   2a. רוּת שָׁכְחָה אֶת הָאַיִל

‏בַּשָּׂדֶה.   2b. רוּת לֹא תִשְׁכַּח אֶת שְׂדוֹת בֹּעַז.   2c. הָאַיִל בַּשָּׂדֶה נִשְׁכַּח.

‏2d. אֵין לָאַיִל אֹכֶל לֶאֱכֹל וּמַיִם לִשְׁתּוֹת כִּי הוּא נִשְׁכָּח.   2e. רוּת זָכְרָה

‏אֶת הָאַיִל בַּשָּׂדֶה בֹּעַז וְהָאַיִל לֹא נִשְׁכַּח.   3a. הַשַּׂר נִלְחַם בַּמִּלְחָמָה.

‏3b. הָיָה דָם עַל חֶרֶב הַשַּׂר אַחֲרֵי הַמִּלְחָמָה.   3c. הַשַּׂר בָּחַר בָּאֲנָשִׁים אֲשֶׁר

‏יִלָּחֲמוּ בַּמִּלְחָמָה.   3d. אַתָּה שַׂר הַחַיִל וְתִלָּחֵם בַּמִּלְחָמָה.   3e. לֹא אֶלָּחֵם

‏בַּמִּלְחָמָה הַזֹּאת כִּי אֲנִי זָקֵן מְאֹד.

‏Exercise 7   1. שׁ.מ.ר - נִפְעַל   2. שׁ.מ.ר - פָּעַל   3. נ.ג.ד -

‏הִפְעִיל   4. ב.י.ן   - הִפְעִיל   5. שׁ.י.ר - פָּעַל   6. נ.ת.ן - פָּעַל

‏7. ל.ק.ח - נִפְעַל .8 ל.ק.ח - פָּעַל .9 ב.ק.שׁ - פָּעֵל .10 ב.נ.ה -

‏פָּעַל .11 ב.ק.שׁ - פָּעֵל .12 צ.ו.ה - פָּעֵל .13 ר.א.ה - פָּעַל

‏14. שׁ.כ.ח - פָּעַל .15 שׁ.כ.ח - פָּעַל, נִפְעַל .16 שׁ.כ.ח - נִפְעַל

‏17. שׁ.כ.ח - נִפְעַל .18 שׁ.כ.ח - נִפְעַל .19 שׁ.כ.ח - פָּעַל

1. being guarded 2. we will guard 3. we will tell 4. we will understand 5. we will sing 6. she gave 7. they were taken 8. we will take 9. I sought 10. I built 11. we will seek 12. we will command 13. we will see 14. I will forget 15. we will forget, he was forgotten 16. being forgotten 17. we will be forgotten 18. you/they will be forgotten 19. you/they will forget

CHAPTER 29

‏Exercise 2   1. A. כִּבַּדְנוּ בְּבֵית לֶחֶם. B. חֲמִשָׁה מְלָכִים כִּבְּדוּ...

‏C. נְשֵׁי מִצְרַיִם כִּבְּדוּ... D. הַחַיִל כִּבַּד... E. כִּבַּדְתָּ... F. בַּת

‏אַבְרָהָם כִּבְּדָה... G. כִּבַּדְתֶּם... H. כִּבַּדְתְּ... I. כִּבַּדְתִּי...

‏J. כִּבַּדְתֶּן... 2. A. דַּעְמִי מְהֻלֶּלֶת כִּי הִיא עָשְׂתָה שָׁלוֹם בֵּין שְׁנֵי

‏הָאַחִים. B. שְׁלֹשָׁה שָׂרִים מְהֻלָּלִים כִּי הֵם עָשׂוּ... C. שְׁתֵּי נְעָרוֹת

‏מְהֻלָּלוֹת כִּי הֵנָּה עָשׂוּ... D. אַתֶּם מְהֻלָּלִים כִּי עֲשִׂיתֶם... E. אַתְּ

‏מְהֻלֶּלֶת כִּי עָשִׂית... F. אֲנִי מְהֻלָּל כִּי עָשִׂיתִי... G. אַתָּה מְהֻלָּל כִּי

‏עָשִׂיתָ... 3. A. הַקָּצֵר יְדַבֵּר עִם הָאִישׁ עַל כַּסְפּוֹ וְיִשָׁלֵּם. B. תְּדַבְּרִי

‏...עַל כַּסְפֵּךְ וּתְשֻׁלְּמִי. C. דִּוַּדְתִּי תְּדַבֵּר...עַל כַּסְפָּהּ וּתְשֻׁלָּם.

‏D. תְּדַבֵּרְנָה...עַל כַּסְפְּכֶן וּתְשֻׁלַּמְנָה. E. תְּדַבֵּר...עַל כַּסְפְּךָ וּתְשֻׁלָּם.

‏F. נְדַבֵּר...עַל כַּסְפֵּנוּ וּנְשֻׁלַּם. G. הַזְּקֵנִים יְדַבְּרוּ...עַל כַּסְפָּם וִישֻׁלְּמוּ

‏H. תְּדַבְּרוּ...עַל כַּסְפְּכֶם וּתְשֻׁלְּמוּ. I. שְׁלֹשׁ הַמִּשְׁפָּחוֹת תְּדַבֵּרְנָה...עַל

‏כַּסְפָּן וּתְשֻׁלַּמְנָה. 4. A. בַּלַּיְלָה הַהוּא נֶחַמְתָּ וְשָׁכַבְתָּ בְּשָׁלוֹם. B. בַּלַּיְלָה

‏הַהוּא נֶחַמְנוּ וְשָׁכַבְנוּ... C. ...רוּחַ נֶחֱמָה וְשָׁכְבָה. D. ...אַנְשֵׁי

‏בֵּית לֶחֶם נֶחֲמוּ וְשָׁכְבוּ... E. ...נֶחַמְתְּ וְשָׁכַבְתְּ... F. ...אַרְבַּע בְּנוֹת

‏מוֹאָב נֶחֲמוּ וְשָׁכְבוּ... G. ...נֶחַמְתֶּם וּשְׁכַבְתֶּם... H. ...נֶחַמְתִּי

70

שְׁנֵי .A .5 ... וְשָׁכְבוּ נֶחֱמוּ נָשִׁים שְׁתַּיִם... .I ... וְשָׁכַבְתִּי

בְּקָשָׁה אַחַת נַעֲרָה .C ... בְּקַשְׁתִּי .B .יִשְׂרָאֵל אֶרֶץ בְּכָל בֻּקְּשׁוּ הַמַּלְאָכִים

הַסְּפָרִים אַרְבַּעַת .F ... בֻּקַּשְׁנוּ .E ... בֻּקְּשׁוּ הַנָּשִׁים חֲמֵשׁ .D ...

... בֻּקְּשׁוּ הִנֵּה .I ... בֻּקְּשׁוּ אֵילִים שְׁלֹשָׁה .H ... בֻּקַּשְׁתֶּן .G ... בֻּקְּשׁוּ

1. The messenger from Jerusalem was honored in Bethlehem.
A. We were honored in Bethlehem. B. Five kings were honored
in Bethlehem. C. The women of Egypt were honored... D. The
army was honored... E. You were honored... F. Abraham's
daughter was honored... G. You were honored... H. You were
honored... I. I was honored... J. You were honored...
2. The man is being praised because he made peace between
the two brothers. A. Naomi is being praised because she
made peace between the two brothers. B. Three officers are
being praised because they made... C. Two maidens are being
praised because they made... D. You are being praised
because you made... E. You are being praised because you
made... F. I am being praised because I made... G. You are
being praised because you made... 3. I will speak with the
man about my money and I will be repaid. A. The harvester
will speak with the man about his money and he will be repaid. B. You will speak...about your money and you will be
repaid. C. My aunt will speak...about her money and she
will be repaid. D. You will speak...about your money and
you will be repaid. E. You will speak...about your money
and you will be repaid. F. We will speak...about our money
and we will be repaid. G. The old ones will speak...about
their money and they will be repaid. H. You will speak...
about your money and you will be repaid. I. The three
families will speak...about their money and they will be
repaid. 4. On that night, Boaz was comforted and he lay
down in peace. A. On that night, you were comforted and you
lay down in peace. B. ...we were comforted and we lay down
... C. ...Ruth was comforted and she lay down... D. ...the
people of Bethlehem were comforted and they lay down...
E. ...you were comforted and you lay down... F. ...four
daughters of Moab were comforted and they lay down...
G. ...you were comforted and you lay down... H. ...I was
comforted and I lay down... I. ...two women were comforted
and they lay down... 5. The chief was sought in all the
land of Israel. A. The two messengers were sought in all
the land of Israel. B. I was sought... C. One maiden was
sought... D. The five women were sought... E. We were
sought... F. The four books were sought... G. You were
sought... H. Three rams were sought.. I. They were sought..

שְׁתֵּי .5 אַחַת .4 חֲמִשָּׁה .3 אַרְבַּעַת .2 שָׁלֹשׁ .1 Exercise 3

שְׁנַיִם .6

1. David loved three women. 2. On that night, the four deeds will be recounted. 3. We are seeing the five tents in the desert. 4. Give me one of your daughters and I will always honor her. 5. There were two wars between Israel and Moab. 6. You will bring one man from the field and two from the city.

Exercise 4   1. שְׁלֹשָׁה אֵילִים   2. מִלְחָמָה אַחַת   3. חֲמִשָּׁה שָׂרִים

4. שְׁתֵּי חֲרָבוֹת   5. אַרְבַּע מִצְוֹת   6. חָמֵשׁ בְּהֵמוֹת   7. שְׁנֵי מִסְפָּרִים

8. אַרְבָּעָה כֵּלִים   9. שָׁבוּעַ אֶחָד   10. שָׁלֹשׁ מִשְׁפָּחוֹת

Exercise 5a   1. הַמֶּלֶךְ יְהֻלָּל.   2. כֶּסֶף שֻׁלַּם.   3. יַיִן נִשְׁפַּךְ.

4. בֵּן יַעֲקֹב בֻּקַּשׁ.   5. אִישָׁהּ נֻחַם.

1. The messenger will praise the king. The king will be praised. 2. The captain repaid him money. Money was repaid. 3. Abraham poured out wine from the vessel. Wine was poured out. 4. Jacob sought his son in all the city. Jacob's son was sought. 5. Ruth comforted her husband. Her husband was comforted.

Exercise 5b   1. הֵנָּה דִּבְּרוּ דִּבְרֵי שָׁלוֹם.   2. תִּזְכְּרוּ אֹתִי וּתְנַחֲמוּ אֹתִי.   3. הֵמָּה פּוֹתְחִים אֶת הַשְּׁעָרִים.   4. שָׁמַעְנוּ אֶת קוֹלוֹ וְזָכַרְנוּ אֶת דְּבָרָיו.

1. Words of peace were spoken to me. They spoke words of peace. 2. I will be remembered and comforted. You will remember and comfort me. 3. The two gates are being opened before me. They are opening the gates. 4. His voice was heard and his words were remembered. We heard his voice and remembered his words.

Exercise 6   1. י.שׁ.ב - פָּעַל   2. שׁ.ו.ב - פָּעַל   3. שׁ.ו.ב - פָּעַל

4. שׁ.ו.ב - הִפְעִיל   5. שׁ.פ.ך - נִפְעַל   6. שׁ.פ.ך - נִפְעַל

7. שׁ.ל.ם - פָּעַל   8. שׁ.ל.ם - פָּעַל   9. ג.נ.ב - פָּעַל   10. ג.נ.ב - נִפְעַל

11. כ.ב.ד - נִפְעַל   12. כ.ב.ד - פָּעַל   13. ד.ב.ר - פָּעַל

14. ג.ד.ל - פָּעַל   15. ג.ד.ל - פָּעַל   16. ג.ד.ל - פָּעַל

17. ג.ד.ל - פָּעַל   18. ג.ד.ל - הִפְעִיל   19. ג.ד.ל - פָּעַל

20. שׁ.ל.ם - פָּעַל

1. he sat 2. he returned/returning 3. we will return 4. we will bring back 5. it was poured out 6. it will be poured out 7. he will be repaid 8. he will repay 9. to be stolen 10. it was stolen 11. she was honored 12. being honored 13. speaking 14. raising 15. she raised 16. they were raised 17. I made great 18. making great 19. being raised 20. being repaid

Exercise 7   1. גּוֹדְלִים 2. מַגְדִּילִים 3. מְגַדְּלִים 4. מְגֻדָּלִים

5. נֶחְמָה 6. נֶחְמָתָ 7. נְנֻחַם 8. נְנַחֵם 9. יְהַלְלוּ 10. יְהֻלְּלוּ

11. בֻּקַּשׁ 12. בִּקֵּשׁ 13. נִלְחַם

1. growing up 2. making great 3. raising 4. being raised 5. you comforted 6. you were comforted 7. we will comfort 8. we will be comforted 9. they will praise 10. they will be praised 11. he sought 12. he was sought 13. he fought

CHAPTER 30

Exercise 2   1. A. הָשְׁלַכְתָּ אֶל תּוֹךְ הַיָּם. B. הָשְׁלַכְנוּ... C. אֵת
וְלֵאָה הָשְׁלַכְתֶּן... D. הָשְׁלַכְתִּי... E. מֵאָה אֲנָשִׁים הָשְׁלְכוּ...
F. הָשְׁלַכְתְּ... G. נַעֲרָה אַחַת הָשְׁלְכָה... H. שֵׁשׁ נָשִׁים רָעוֹת הָשְׁלְכוּ...
I. הָשְׁלַכְתֶּם... 2. A. עַתָּה אֲנִי מָמְלַךְ עַל כָּל הָאָרֶץ מֵהֶהָרִים עַד הַיַּרְדֵּן.
B. עַתָּה הַשַּׂר מָמְלַךְ... C. עַתָּה אַתְּ מָמְלֶכֶת... D. עַתָּה אַתֶּן מָמְלָכוֹת..
E. עַתָּה שְׁמֹנַת הַשֹּׁפְטִים מָמְלָכִים... F. עַתָּה אֲנַחְנוּ מָמְלָכִים... G. עַתָּה
לֵאָה מָמְלֶכֶת... H. עַתָּה אַתָּה מָמְלָךְ... I. עַתָּה תֵּשַׁע בְּנוֹת רִבְקָה
מָמְלָכוֹת... 3. A. הָאַיִל יֻשְׁלַךְ מֵרֹאשׁ הָהָר. B. הַחֶרֶב תֻּשְׁלַךְ...
C. רָחֵל וּמִרְיָם תֻּשְׁלַכְנָה... D. תֻּשְׁלַךְ... E. בָּשְׁלַךְ... 4. A. בְּפַעַם
הַזֹּאת אֶשָּׁפֵט בְּבֵית לֶחֶם. B. אַתְּ וְרִבְקָה תִּשָּׁפֵטְנָה... C. הַגּוֹי...
וְיִשָּׁפֵט... D. ...נִשָּׁפֵט... E. ...תִּשָּׁפְטִי... F. רָחֵל...תִּשָּׁפֵט...
G. ...תִּשָּׁפְטוּ... H. ...תִּשָּׁפֵט... 5. A. לֵאָה וְרָחֵל לֹא הֵבִינוּ אֶת
דִּבְרֵי הַמַּלְאָךְ. B. לֹא הֵבַנְתָּ... C. לֹא הֲבִינוֹתֶן... D. לֹא הֲבִינֹנוּ...
E. שְׁנֵי דּוֹדַי לֹא הֵבִינוּ... F. לֹא הֲבִינוֹתֶם... G. רֹאשׁ הָעִיר לֹא

Chapter 30

הָבִין ... H. לֹא הֲבַנְתְּ ... I. לֹא הֲבִינוֹתִי ... A. 6. רִבְקָה שָׂמָה אֶת

הָאֹכֶל וְאֶת הַמַּיִם לְפָנֶיהָ וְשָׁתִית וְאָכְלְתָּ. B. ... לִפְנֵיכֶן וּשְׁתִיתֶן

וַאֲכַלְתֶּן. C. ... לִפְנֵיהֶם וְהֵם שָׁתוּ וְאָכְלוּ. D. ... לְפָנֶיהָ וְשָׁתִית

וְאָכְלְתָּ. E. ... לְפָנֵינוּ וְשָׁתִינוּ וַאֲכַלְנוּ. F. ... לִפְנֵיהֶן וְהֵנָּה שָׁתוּ

וְאָכְלוּ. G. ... לְפָנָיו וְהוּא שָׁתָה וְאָכַל. H. ... לִפְנֵיכֶם וּשְׁתִיתֶם

וַאֲכַלְתֶּם. I. ... לְפָנֶיהָ וְהִיא שָׁתְתָה וְאָכְלָה.

1. The silver was thrown into the midst of the sea. A. You were thrown into the midst of the sea. B. We were thrown... C. You and Leah were thrown... D. I was thrown... E. A hundred men were thrown... F. You were thrown... G. One maiden was thrown... H. Six evil women were thrown... I. You were thrown... 2. Now you are being made kings over all the land from the mountains to the Jordan. A. Now I am being made king over all the land from the mountains to the Jordan. B. Now the officer is being made king... C. Now you are being made ruler... D. Now you are being made rulers... E. Now the eight judges are being made kings... F. Now we are being made kings... G. Now Leah is being made ruler... H. Now you are being made king... I. Now Rebecca's nine daughters are being made rulers... 3. A thousand stones will be thrown from the top of the mountain. A. The ram will be thrown from the top of the mountain. B. The sword will be thrown... C. Rachel and Miriam will be thrown... D. You will be thrown... E. We will be thrown... 4. At this time, he will be judged in Bethlehem. A. At this time, I will be judged in Bethlehem. B. At this time, you and Rebecca will be judged... C. ...the nation will be judged.. D. ...we will be judged... E. ...you will be judged... F. ...Rachel will be judged... G. ...you will be judged... H. ...you will be judged... 5. Miriam did not understand the words of the messenger. A. Leah and Rachel did not understand the words of the messenger. B. You did not understand... C. You did not understand... D. We did not understand... E. My two uncles did not understand... F. You did not understand... G. The head of the city did not understand... H. You did not understand... I. I did not understand... 6. Rebecca put the food and the water before me, and I drank and ate. A. Rebecca put the food and the water before you, and you drank and ate. B. ...before you, and you drank and ate. C. ...before them, and they drank and ate. D. ...before you, and you drank and ate. E. ...before us, and we drank and ate. F. ...before them, and they drank and ate. G. ...before him, and he drank and ate. H. ...before you, and you drank and ate. I. ...before her, and she ate and drank.

Exercise 3 1. תֵּשַׁע 2. שְׁמֹנָה 3. חָמֵשׁ 4. שָׁלֹשׁ 5. שֶׁבַע

6. מָאתַיִם 7. שֵׁשׁ 8. עֶשֶׂר 9. אַרְבַּע 10. אַחַת 11. שְׁתַּיִם

12. אַלְפַּיִם

Exercise 4 1. שֵׁשֶׁת 2. עֶשֶׂר 3. שִׁבְעָה 4. תֵּשַׁע 5. שְׁמֹנַת

1. We will trust Rachel and her six brothers. 2. You counted ten animals in the field. 3. I will rescue seven people because I am a mighty man of valor. 4. The officer will give nine swords to the judge. 5. You took the eight vessels of water from the lads and they could not drink.

Exercise 5 1. הַשַּׂר הַמְלַךְ. 2. אֲבָנִים מֻשְׁלָכִים. 3. הַזָּהָב יִגָּנֵב.

4. מַלְאֲכֵי הַמֶּלֶךְ נִשְׁלָחוּ. 5. הַבָּנוֹת תִּלְבַּשְׁנָה.

1. The army of Moab made its chief king after the battle. The chief was made king. 2. Rebecca and Miriam are throwing stones into the midst of the Jordan. Stones are being thrown. 3. You will steal the gold from the tabernacle in the evening. The gold will be stolen. 4. A hundred times we sent the king's messengers to Jerusalem. The king's messengers were sent. 5. Leah will dress her daughters in the morning. Her daughters will be dressed.

Exercise 6 1a. שְׁלֹשֶׁת הַשֹּׁפְטִים הָלְכוּ אֶל יְרוּשָׁלַם. 2a. אַרְבַּעַת

הַשֹּׁפְטִים לָקְחוּ אֶת הַפְּרִי אֶל יְרוּשָׁלַם. 3a. הַפְּרִי נִשְׁלַח אֶל אַנְשֵׁי

יְרוּשָׁלַם. 4a. הַפְּרִי יִשָּׁלַח אֶל שִׁבְעָה שׁוֹפְטִים בִּירוּשָׁלַם. 5a. פְּרִי

נִלְקַח מֵהָעֵץ וְנִשְׁלַח אֶל שְׁמֹנַת הַשּׁוֹפְטִים. 1b. לְשָׂרָה שְׁנַיִם בְּעָלִים.

2b. רָחֵל בָּחֲרָה אֶת הַבְּעָלִים הָאֵלֶּה הַיּוֹם. 3b. שֵׁשׁ בָּשִׁים מִמִּשְׁפַּחַת שָׂרָה

נִבְחֲרוּ כִּי הֵנָּה חֲכָמוֹת. 4b. שָׂרָה חֲכָמָה מֵחֲמֵשׁ הַבָּשִׁים בְּבֵיתָהּ.

5b. שְׁמֹנָה בָשִׁים מִמּוֹאָב תִּבְחַרְנָה בִּבְגָדִים מִירוּשָׁלַם. 1c. בֶּן יַעֲקֹב סָפַר

עֲשָׂרָה אֵילִים. 2c. תֵּשַׁע בָּנֵי יַעֲקֹב יִסְפְּרוּ אֶת הָאֵילִים בָּהָר.

3c. יַעֲקֹב לֹא יוּכַל לִסְפֹּר אֶת הָאֵילִים בָּהָר. 4c. יַעֲקֹב לֹא שָׁכַח כִּי

הוּא רָאָה אֶלֶף אֵילִים בָּהָר. 5c. הָהָר בִּיהוּדָה לֹא נִשְׁכַּח כִּי הוּא פֹּהָר

בְּמוֹאָב.

Exercise 7 1. מָלַכְתֶּם 2. הִמְלַכְתֶּם 3. הָמְלַכְתֶּם 4. תִּמְלֹכְנָה

5. תַּמְלַכְנָה 6. תַּמְלִכְנָה 7. זָכַרְתִּי 8. נִזְכַּרְתִּי 9. הִזְכַּרְתִּי

10. זוֹכֶרֶת

1. you ruled 2. you made king 3. you were made kings 4. you will rule 5. you will make king 6. you will be made rulers 7. I remembered 8. I was remembered 9. I reminded 10. remembering

CHAPTER 31

Exercise 2 1. A. עוֹדְךָ מִתְפַּלֵּל עַל הַשָּׁלוֹם יוֹם יוֹם. B. עוֹדֶנּוּ מִתְפַּלְלִים... C. עוֹדֶנּוּ מִתְפַּלֵּל... D. עוֹדָהּ מִתְפַּלֶּלֶת... E. עוֹדָם מִתְפַּלְלִים... F. עוֹדָן מִתְפַּלֶּלֶת... 2. A. אַרְבַּעַת בְּנֵי הַשּׁוֹפֵט הִתְהַלְּלוּ וְלֹא הִלְלוּ אֶת עֲבַד עֲבָדֵיהֶם. B. בַּת הַנָּבִיא הִתְהַלְּלָה וְלֹא הִלְלָה... עֲבָדֶיהָ. C. הִתְהַלַּלְתֶּן וְלֹא הִלַּלְתֶּן...עֲבָדֵיכֶן. D. הִתְהַלַּלְנוּ וְלֹא הִלַּלְנוּ...עֲבָדֵינוּ. E. הִתְהַלַּלְתִּי וְלֹא הִלַּלְתִּי...עֲבָדִי. F. הִתְהַלַּלְתְּ וְלֹא הִלַּלְתְּ...עֲבָדַיִךְ. G. נְשֵׁי הַשַּׂר הִתְהַלְּלוּ וְלֹא הִלְלוּ...עֲבָדֵיהֶן. H. הִתְהַלַּלְתֶּם וְלֹא הִלַּלְתֶּם...עֲבָדֵיכֶם. I. הִתְהַלַּלְתָּ וְלֹא הִלַּלְתָּ...עֲבָדֶיהָ. 3. A. תִּתְבַּחֲמָה כַּאֲשֶׁר תִּרְאֶינָה אֶת עֲבַד בְּנֵיכֶן הַטּוֹבִים. B. אֶתְנַחֵם כַּאֲשֶׁר אֶרְאֶה...בָּנַי. C. רִבְקָה תִּתְנַחֵם כַּאֲשֶׁר תִּרְאֶה...בָּנֶיהָ... D. הַנָּבִיא יִתְנַחֵם כַּאֲשֶׁר יִרְאֶה...בָּנָיו. E. שִׁבְעַת הָאָבוֹת יִתְנַחֲמוּ...יִרְאוּ...בְּנֵיהֶם. F. תִּתְנַחֲמוּ כַּאֲשֶׁר תִּרְאוּ...בְּנֵיכֶם. G. נִתְנַחֵם כַּאֲשֶׁר נִרְאֶה...בָּנֵינוּ. H. תִּתְנַחֲמִי כַּאֲשֶׁר תִּרְאִי...בָּנַיִךְ... I. תֵּשַׁע הַמִּשְׁפָּחוֹת תִּתְנַחֵמְנָה כַּאֲשֶׁר תִּרְאֶינָה...בְּנֵיהֶן. 4. A. הַנָּבִיא יְדַבֵּר אֶת הָאֱמֶת וְלֹא אָשִׂים לְבִּי אֵלָיו. B. ...וְזֶרַע אַבְרָהָם לֹא יָשִׂים לִבּוֹ אֵלָיו. C. ...נַחֲמֵשֶׁת הַשָּׂרִים לֹא יָשִׂימוּ לִבָּם אֵלָיו. D. ...וְלֹא תָּשִׂימוּ לִבְּכֶם אֵלָיו. E. ...וְלֹא תָּשִׂימִי לִבֵּךְ אֵלָיו. F. ...נִשְׁלֹשׁ הַבָּנוֹת לֹא תָּשֵׂמְנָה לִבָּן אֵלָיו. G. ...וְלֹא נָשִׂים לְבָנוּ אֵלָיו. H. ...וְלֹא תָּשִׂים לִבְּךָ אֵלָיו. I. ...וְהָעֶבֶד לֹא יָשִׂים לִבּוֹ אֵלָיו. 5. A. צִוִּית אֶת בִּנְךָ לֵאמֹר

"לֵךְ נָא אֶל הַמִּדְבָּר לְהִתְפַּלֵּל תְּפִלּוֹת וְלִרְאוֹת אֶת הָעֲבוֹדָה בְּמִשְׁכָּן."

B. צִוִּינוּ אֶת בָּנֵינוּ לֵאמֹר: "לְךָ... C. שָׂרָה צִוְּתָה אֶת בְּנָהּ לֵאמֹר: "לְךְ

... D. שֵׁשׁ הַשּׁוֹמְרִים צִוּוּ אֶת בְּנֵיהֶם לֵאמֹר: "לְכוּ... E. צִוִּיתֶן אֶת

בְּנֵיכֶן לֵאמֹר: "לְכוּ... F. צִוִּיתִי אֶת בָּנַי לֵאמֹר: "לְךָ... G. צִוִּיתָ

אֶת בִּנְךָ לֵאמֹר: "לְךְ... H. שְׁתֵּי נָשִׁים צִוּוּ אֶת בְּנֵיהֶן לֵאמֹר: "לְכוּ...

I. צִוִּיתֶם אֶת בְּנֵיכֶם לֵאמֹר: "לְכוּ...

1. I am still praying about peace daily. A. You are still
praying about peace daily. B. We are still praying... C. He
is still praying... D. She is still praying... E. They are
still praying... F. You are still praying... 2. The king
praised himself and did not praise the labor of his servants. A. The judge's four sons praised themselves and did
not praise the labor of their servants. B. The daughter of
the prophet praised herself and did not praise...her servants. C. You praised yourselves and did not praise...your
servants. D. We praised ourselves and did not praise...our
servants. E. I praised myself and did not praise...my servants. F. You praised yourself and did not praise...your
servants. G. The chief's wives praised themselves and did
not praise...their servants. H. You praised yourselves and
did not praise...your servants. I. You praised yourself and
did not praise...your servants. 3. You will comfort yourself when you see the service of your good sons. A. You
will comfort yourselves when you see the service of your
good sons. B. I will comfort myself when I see...my good
sons. C. Rebecca will comfort herself when she sees...her
good sons. D. The prophet will comfort himself when he sees
...his good sons. E. The seven fathers will comfort themselves when they see...their good sons. F. You will comfort
yourselves when you see...your good sons. G. We will comfort ourselves when we see...our good sons. H. You will
comfort yourself when you see...your good sons. I. The nine
families will comfort themselves when they see...their good
sons. 4. The prophet will speak the truth and the men will
not pay attention to him. A. The prophet will speak the
truth and I will not pay attention to him. B. ...and the
offspring of Abraham will not pay attention to him. C. ...
and the five officers will not pay attention to him. D. ...
and you will not pay attention to him. E. ...and you will
not pay attention to him. F. ...and the three daughters
will not pay attention to him. G. ...and we will not pay
attention to him. H. ...and you will not pay attention to
him. I. ...and the servant will not pay attention to him.
5. The father commanded his son, saying: "Please go to the
wilderness to pray prayers and to see the work at the

tabernacle." A. You commanded your son, saying: "Please go
to the wilderness to pray prayers and to see the work at
the tabernacle." B. We commanded our son, saying: "Please
go... C. Sarah commanded her son, saying: "Please go...
D. The six guards commanded their sons, saying: "Please go
... E. You commanded your sons, saying: "Please go...
F. I commanded my son, saying: "Please go... G. You commanded your son, saying: "Please go... H. Two women commanded their sons, saying: "Please go... I. You commanded
your sons, saying: "Please go...

Exercise 3 1. שְׁמַעְתֶּם, שׁוֹמְעִים, תִּשְׁמְעוּ, שָׁמוֹעַ שְׁמַעְתֶּם, שָׁמוֹעַ תִּשְׁמְעוּ

3. בּוֹאִי 2. רָאִיתִי, רוֹאֶה, אֶרְאֶה, רָאֹה רָאִיתִי, רָאֹה אֶרְאֶה שִׁמְעוּ,

5. נִלְחֲמוּ 4. הִשְׁלִיךְ, מַשְׁלִיהַ, יַשְׁלִיךְ, הַשְׁלֵךְ הִשְׁלִיךְ, הַשְׁלֵךְ יַשְׁלִיךְ

6. הִתְפַּלְּלוּ, יִתְפַּלְלוּ 7. שׁוּב 8. עָשָׂה, עוֹשֶׂה, יַעֲשֶׂה, עָשֹׂה עָשָׂה, עָשֹׂה

יַעֲשֶׂה

1. You (heard, are hearing, will hear, surely heard, surely
will hear, hear!) the words from the mouth of your offspring. 2. I (saw, am seeing, will see, really saw, will
really see) the place where these judgements were written.
3. (Come!) please before the judge to hear his judgement.
4. The servant (threw, is throwing, will throw, really
threw, will really throw) the tree into the midst of the
sea. 5. At the time of the famine, the men of Canaan
(fought) against the people of Israel, and they took them
as slaves to their land. 6. Thus they (prayed, will pray)
many prayers at that time. 7. Thus said the prophet to
David: "(Return!) please with your offspring to the land of
Israel." 8. The judge (made, is making, will make, surely
made, surely will make) a judgement all the days of his
life.

Exercise 4 1. נָחַם 2. יַזְכִּיר 3. הִלְלוּ 4. מַגְדִּיל 5. הַמְלִיכוּ

6. שׁוּב

1. He heard the prayer of his slave and he comforted him.
2. The prophet will remind the king that he must keep the
commandments. 3. The nine old men praised the deeds of the
mighty man of valor. 4. Now the king is making my name
great in all the land because I saved my people from the
hand of Moab. 5. Thus said the prophet: "Crown a king from
the offspring of David." 6. The father commanded his son,
saying: "Please return to my land."

78

Exercise 5 1. מַה הִגַּדְתָּ לָעֶבֶד? 2. הִגַּדְתִּי לָעֶבֶד לְהָבִיא אֶת הַכֵּלִים.
3. תַּגִּיד לַעֲבָדִים לְהָבִיא אֶת הַלֶּחֶם וְאֶת הַיַּיִן. 4. הָעֲבָדִים הֵבִיאוּ אֶת הַלֶּחֶם וְאֶת הַיַּיִן אֶל בֵּית הַמֶּלֶךְ. 5. נָשִׂים אֶת הַלֶּחֶם וְאֶת הַיַּיִן לִפְנֵי הַמֶּלֶךְ.

Exercise 7 1. אֶגְנֹב 2. אֶגָּנֵב 3. אֶתְכַּבֵּד 4. גֻּנַּב 5. נִגְנַב
6. הִתְכַּבֵּד 7. בָּאוּ 8. הֵבִיאוּ 9. בּוֹאוּ 10. הָבִיאוּ 11. מְנַחֵם
12. מְחֻנָּחֶם 13. תִּסְפְּרִי 14. תְּסֻפְּרִי 15. עָלְתָה 16. לָקְחוּ
17. נִלְקְחוּ 18. יָקְחוּ 19. יִלָּקְחוּ 20. קַחַת 21. הֻלְקַח
22. זוֹכְרוֹת 23. מַזְכִּירוֹת 24. נִזְכָּרוֹת

CHAPTER 32

Exercise 2. 1. A. יְרַדְתֶּם אֶל הַיָּם וּמְצָאתֶם שָׁם אֶת הַנָּבִיא. B. יָרַדְתָּ אֶל הַיָּם וּמָצָאתָ... C. עֶבֶד אֶחָד יָרַד...וּמָצָא... D. רָחֵל וְרִבְקָה יָרְדוּ...וּמָצְאוּ... E. ...יָרַדְנוּ...וּמְצָאנוּ... F. עֲשֶׂרֶת הַשּׁוֹפְטִים יָרְדוּ...וּמָצְאוּ... G. ...יָרַדְתִּי...וּמָצָאתִי... H. ...יְרַדְתֶּן...וּמְצָאתֶן... I. ...יָרַדְתְּ...וּמָצָאת...
2. A. אִם אֶלֵךְ עַל הָאֲבָנִים, אֶפֹּל. B. אִם אַהֲרֹן וְיוֹסֵף יֵלְכוּ...יִפֹּלוּ. C. אִם הַזְּקֵנָה תֵּלֵךְ...תִּפֹּל. D. אִם חֲמֵשׁ הַבָּנוֹת תֵּלַכְנָה...תִּפֹּלְנָה. E. אִם תֵּלְכוּ...תִּפֹּלוּ. F. אִם אֲחִי מֹשֶׁה יֵלֵךְ...יִפֹּל. G. אִם גֵּלֵךְ...נִפֹּל. H. אִם תֵּלֵךְ...תִּפֹּל. I. אִם תֵּלַכְנָה...תִּפֹּלְנָה.
3. A. רִבְקָה יָצְאָה מִן הָאֹהֶל בַּבֹּקֶר וְקָרְאָה לְבָנֶיהָ. B. שֵׁשֶׁת הַשָּׂרִים יָצְאוּ וְקָרְאוּ לִבְנֵיהֶם. C. הַגִּבּוֹר יָצָא...וְקָרָא לְבָנָיו. D. יָצָאתִי...וְקָרָאתִי לְבָנַי. E. יְצָאתֶם...וּקְרָאתֶם לִבְנֵיכֶם. F. יָצָאנוּ...וְקָרָאנוּ לְבָנֵינוּ. G. יָצָאתָ...וְקָרָאתָ לְבָנֶיךָ. H. יְצָאתֶן...וּקְרָאתֶן לִבְנֵיכֶן. I. מִרְיָם וְלֵאָה יָצְאוּ...וְקָרְאוּ לִבְנֵיהֶן.
4. A. כַּאֲשֶׁר הָעֲבָדִים עוֹמְדִים לִפְנֵי הַמֶּלֶךְ, הֵמָּה מְבִיאִים אֵלָיו מִנְחָה. B. כַּאֲשֶׁר רִבְקָה עוֹמֶדֶת...הִיא מְבִיאָה... C. כַּאֲשֶׁר אַתָּה עוֹמֵד...אַתָּה מֵבִיא... D. כַּאֲשֶׁר אֲנַחְנוּ

79

עוֹמְדִים...מְבִיאִים ... E. כַּאֲשֶׁר אַבְרָהָם עוֹמֵד...מֵבִיא...מֵבִיא ... F. כַּאֲשֶׁר

הִנֵּה עוֹמְדוֹת...מְבִיאוֹת... A. 5. אוֹצִיא אֶת הַכֶּסֶף מִבֵּיתִי וַאֲשַׁלֵּם לְשָׂרַי

B. הוֹדוּ יוֹצִיא...מִבֵּיתוֹ וִישַׁלֵּם לְשָׂרָיו. C. אִמִּי תּוֹצִיא...מִבֵּיתָהּ

וּתְשַׁלֵּם לְשָׂרֶיהָ. D. שְׁתֵּי בָנוֹת תּוֹצֶאנָה...מִבֵּיתָן וּתְשַׁלֵּמְנָה לְשָׂרֵיהֶן.

E. תּוֹצִיא...מִבֵּיתְךָ וּתְשַׁלֵּם לְשָׂרֶיךָ. F. מַלְאֲכֵי הַמֶּלֶךְ יוֹצִיאוּ...מִבֵּיתָם

וִישַׁלְּמוּ לְשָׂרֵיהֶם. G. נוֹצִיא...מִבֵּיתֵנוּ וּנְשַׁלֵּם לְשָׂרֵנוּ. H. תּוֹצִיאוּ...

מִבֵּיתְכֶם וּתְשַׁלְּמוּ לְשָׂרֵיכֶם. I. תּוֹצִיאִי...מִבֵּיתֵךְ וּתְשַׁלְּמִי לְשָׂרַיִךְ.

6. A. אֶעֱלֶה אֶל רֹאשׁ הָהָר וּמִשָּׁם אֶרְאֶה אֶת הַיָּם. B. מֵאָה נָשִׁים תַּעֲלֶינָה

...וְתִרְאֶינָה... C. שָׂרֵי הַמֶּלֶךְ יַעֲלוּ...וְיִרְאוּ... D. תַּעֲלוּ...וְתִרְאוּ...

E. מִרְיָם תַּעֲלֶה...וְתִרְאֶה... F. תַּעֲלִי...וְתִרְאִי... G. נַעֲלֶה...

וְנִרְאֶה... H. הָעֶבֶד יַעֲלֶה...וְיִרְאֶה... I. תַּעֲלֶינָה...וְתִרְאֶינָה...

1. Miriam went down to the sea and found the prophet there.
A. You went down to the sea and found the prophet there.
B. You went down...and found... C. One servant went down...
and found... D. Rachel and Rebecca went down...and found...
E. We went down...and found... F. The ten judges went down..
and found... G. I went down...and found... H. You went down
...and found... I. You went down...and found... 2. If you
walk upon the stones, you will fall. A. If I walk upon the
stones, I will fall. B. If Aaron and Joseph walk...they will
fall. C. If the old woman walks...she will fall. D. If the
five daughters walk...they will fall. E. If you walk...you
will fall. F. If the brother of Moses walks...he will fall.
G. If we walk...we will fall. H. If you walk...you will fall
I. If you walk...you will fall. 3. You came out of the tent
in the morning and called to your sons. A. Rebecca came out
of the tent in the morning and called to her sons. B. The
six chiefs came out...and called to their sons. C. The
mighty man came out...and called to his sons. D. I came out
...and called to my sons. E. You came out...and called to
your sons. F. We came out...and called to our sons. G. You
came out...and called to your sons. H. You came out...and
called to your sons. I. Miriam and Leah came out...and
called to their sons. 4. When you stand before the king, you
bring a gift to him. A. When the slaves stand before the
king, they bring a gift to him. B. When Rebecca stands
before the king, she brings... C. When you stand...you bring
... D. When we stand...we bring... E. When Abraham stands..
he brings... F. When they stand...they bring... 5. Sarah
will bring out the money from her house and will repay her

officers. A. I will bring out the money from my house and will repay my officers. B. His uncle will bring out...his house and will repay his officers. C. My mother...her house and will repay her officers. D. Two daughters...their house and will repay their officers. E. You will bring out...your house and will repay your officers. F. The king's messengers will bring out...their house and will repay their officers. G. We will bring out...our house and will repay our officers H. You will bring out...your house and will repay your officers. I. You will bring out...your house and will repay your officers. 6. You will go up to the top of the mountain and from there you will see the sea. A. I will go up to the top of the mountain and from there I will see the sea. B. A hundred women will go up...they will see... C. The king's officers will go up...they will see... D. You will go up... you will see... E. Miriam will go up...she will see... F. You will go up...you will see... G. We will go up...we will see... H. The slave will go up...he will see... I. You will go up...you will see...

Exercise 3 1. נָפְלָה 2. יָצָאתִי, וְהָלַכְתִּי 3. יָלְדָה 4. גָּאַל

5. מָצָאתָ 6. נָשְׂאָה 7. עָמַדְנוּ 8. עָשִׂיתִי

1. Ruth fell from the tree. 2. I went out of the house and walked to my uncle's house. 3. Rebecca gave birth to two sons and one daughter. 4. Joseph redeemed the field of his brother. 5. You found the food in the vessel. 6. The animal carried the water. 7. We stood with the women of Moab to see the king. 8. I regularly did good deeds.

Exercise 4 1. אוֹצִיא 2. יַעֲבִיד 3. תּוֹרִידוּ 4. יוֹלִיד

5. נַעֲמִיד 6. תַּצִּיל 7. תַּגִּידִי 8. תּוֹשִׁיבוּ

1. I will bring out all the clothes from my tent. 2. The chief will cause his slaves to work. 3. You will bring down fruit from the tree. 4. Isaac will beget two sons. 5. We will set up the vessels in the tabernacle. 6. You will save your brother from the hand of the king of Moab. 7. You will tell us everything that is written in the book. 8. You will seat me on a great chair.

Exercise 5 1. נִגְאֲלוּ, יִגָּאֲלוּ 2. נִקְרָאתִי, אֶקָּרֵא 3. נִמְצָאתֶם,

4. נוֹלַד, יִוָּלֵד 5. נִבְנוּ, יִבָּנוּ 6. נָשְׂאוּ, יִנָּשְׂאוּ תִּמָּצְאוּ

1. The children of Israel (were redeemed, will be redeemed) from Egypt. 2. I (was called, will be called) to the king today. 3. You (were found, will be found) in your house in the evening. 4. He (was born, will be born) in Bethlehem.

81

5. The dwelling places (were built, will be built) in the desert. 6. The water (was carried, will be carried) in vessels to the field.

Exercise 6   1. מ.צ.א - נִפְעַל   2. ר.א.ה - פָּעַל   3. ז.כ.ר - הִפְעִיל

4. נ.פ.ל - פָּעַל   5. י.ד.ע - הִפְעִיל   6. מ.ל.ך - הִפְעִיל   7. ק.ו.ם

8. ל.ק.ח - פָּעַל   9. י.צ.א - הִפְעִיל   10. י.ל.ד - הִפְעִיל

11. י.שׁ.ב - פָּעַל   12. נ.ג.ד - הִפְעִיל   13. י.ר.ד - הִפְעִיל

14. מ.צ.א - פָּעַל   15. ק.ר.א - נִפְעַל   16. י.צ.א - פָּעַל   17. ע.שׂ.ה

18. פָּעַל - ע.ל.ה   19. א.כ.ל - הִפְעִיל   20. נ.צ.ל - פָּעַל - הִפְעִיל

82